The

Heroic

Venture

■

A Parable of

Project

Leadership

■

Don

Allsman

Contents

References

F o r e w o r d

"All I can say is that it's about time!" This statement summarizes my sentiment on the importance and value of this important text on project management for urban workers on the adventure of strategic thinking and living. Don Allsman, my friend and colleague in developing urban leaders, has done a great service to the urban church by writing a clear and compelling account on the wisdom of project management. The challenges facing those who have been called to represent Christ in urban America are fierce, numerous, and thorny. Only the most careful and prepared minds will be able to engage in projects designed to advance the Kingdom of God in the city and take advantage of the scarce resources and dramatic opportunities present there. *The Heroic Venture* will be an important tool to equip urban leaders and others in the skills, mindsets, and practices of project management.

Using the remarkable "project" of Lewis and Clark as a backdrop for its insights into strategic planning and living, *The Heroic Venture* argues not only about the nuts-and-bolts of good project management but also gets at the fundamental dispositions and deeper commitments that underlie it. The book is aptly titled, for all successful project management is, in fact, a venture. What makes this kind of planning and practice heroic in my judgment is precisely what is covered in this text. This is a text written with those people in mind whose lives are a continual and unbroken series of heartaches, shortages, and tribulations, which are part and parcel of doing effective urban mission in America's hurting inner city communities. I count all of those who serve Christ in the city as authentic heroes, whose faithful service and courageous engagement of the powers in the city will win them both the praise and reward of the Savior whom they so nobly serve. Indeed, each of them is living out the heroic venture mapped out for them by our Lord to make disciples of Jesus Christ in urban America.

As a scholar, missionary educator, and city-born saint, I have for some time believed that we have needed a clear and compelling account of the wisdom of project management, written with urban workers in mind. For years, I cajoled, challenged, and complained to Don that he should write a piece on project management designed for use as a textbook with urban Christian leaders. Since this system was developed by the military and the construction and aerospace industries, and since Don had experience in these domains, he was, in my mind, the perfect candidate to write it! Of course, the science of project management has exploded in secular business arenas, demonstrated by the amazing growth and influence of the Project Management Institute, and the ever-growing and voluminous store of books on the subject. Don's important work not only adds to that store, but it uniquely addresses the perspectives, principles, and priorities of those who can adapt these liberating techniques to minister effectively as Christ's servants among the poor in the city.

One of the truly refreshing characteristics of *The Heroic Venture* is its biblical foundation and argument. In a real sense, this is a text anchored on the wisdom to be gleaned from a careful and critical reading of the projects in the Bible. Of particular interest to me is the way in which Don has woven the accounts of numerous biblical projects into this work. Through them, he effectively drives home the point that wisdom, in the final analysis, belongs to God, who is its author and dispenser. Don's keen ability to analyze these events, and interpret them in such a way as to get at the heart of the matter in each case, is wonderful to watch and terribly beneficial. At the same time, *The Heroic Venture* is not pollyannaish nor naive; it takes hard work, dedication, ingenuity, and tenacity to accomplish the high purposes of God in the lives of those called to ministry. The ability to look difficulty full in the face and yet to endure and persevere is in large part a driving theme of this wonderful text, which is why it is so important for those working cross-culturally among the poor. Those making disciples in the city among the poor do, in fact, have the storehouse of God's wisdom and knowledge at their disposal.

I commend *The Heroic Venture* to you for what it is and what it can become. It is, without question, one of the finest books on project management I have ever read, which is informed by my own sizable library on the subject. But, more than that, it is a personal challenge to excellence, greatness and vision by someone I have seen live it out time after time in his own unique and powerful journey as my colleague in training urban missionaries and leaders. What this text can become for you is a springboard, a goad, a jolt to begin to live out the venture that the Spirit has for you to accomplish, the one which according to St. Paul is greater than you can ask or think (Eph. 3.20). God does not call us to do what our abilities warrant but what his will and purposes dictate. Everyone who has ever accomplished great things for God has set out on their own unique heroic venture, their own personal path to greatness, courage, and accomplishment. My sincere desire is that *The Heroic Venture* will prompt you to do great things for God, and to receive great grace from God, in order that you may give great glory to God.

Rev. Dr. Don L. Davis
October 24, 2006

Introduction

*Do not be slothful in zeal, be fervent in spirit,
serve the Lord.* ~ Romans 12.11

*Desire without knowledge is not good, and whoever makes
haste with his feet misses his way.* ~ Proverbs 19.2

YOU HAVE a burden, a dream, or an idea. You cannot get it off your mind. You think it is something God wants you to do but you do not know what to do next. Your dream might be big or small: start a children's ministry, plant a church, conduct a vacation Bible class, develop a ministry for drug addicts, start a homeless ministry, or launch a single mother's home. The purpose of this book is to inspire you to pursue your vision with wisdom and passion until that vision becomes a reality. My prayer is that you will be set on fire by God as he guides you through your own Heroic Venture.

You are not the first to have an idea for ministry welling up within you. God has been leading people to start new ministries and projects since the creation of Adam and Eve. Even before the Fall, God was giving assignments to people. Adam and Eve were given the task to rule over the earth and name the animals of God's creation (Gen. 3.19).

There have been many other specific assignments that God has given his people throughout biblical history:

⋄ *Noah (build an ark)*

⋄ *Moses (lead the exodus)*

⋄ *Joshua (conquer the Promised Land)*

⋄ *Gideon (defeat the Midianites)*

⋄ *Nehemiah (rebuild the wall)*

⋄ *Joseph and Mary (raise the Messiah)*

⋄ *Jesus (make sacrifice for sin)*

⋄ *Paul and Barnabas (evangelize the Gentiles)*

⋄ *Peter (preach to Cornelius).*

In my study of the Scriptures, I have identified thirty specific projects that men and women carried out in response to God (see Reference H, at the back of this book). While there are dozens of great Bible stories, I have limited myself these thirty projects to make the points in this book. As you consider what God has called you to do, you can learn much from their example.

An Uncertain Journey

The people God selects for kingdom ministry are often unlikely candidates. Some were surprised at their call and asked God to select someone else. When God gives his people a burden for kingdom ministry they must be ready for difficulty and uncertainty. Even though God helped them complete the task, it was never easy, but full of challenges. In warfare, the military has a term called *friction*. It means, "things seldom go according to plan." In ministry, things *never* go according to plan. Even when God is clearly behind a venture, ministry leaders must expect difficulty; a zigzag way to the finish. When you accept the Heroic Venture, both wisdom and passion must be exercised in order to overcome the obstacles ahead.

A Parable of Project Leadership

I have chosen the epic story of the Lewis and Clark Expedition to serve as a parable for *The Heroic Venture*. I did not choose their voyage because the members are examples of godliness, nor do I maintain that they are even followers of Jesus. Lewis and Clark had many moral failings. But theirs is a classic story of a huge undertaking into the unknown, and it provides a fascinating illustration of *seeing vision turn into reality*. The expedition, whose members were called the "Corps of Discovery," is an amazing account of pursuing a vision into uncharted waters. The excursion has much to show us about *wise and passionate* project leadership.

Another reason to use the Lewis and Clark saga is the variety of cross-cultural encounters they experienced with various Native American tribes. The differences in language and culture forced the expedition to work at cultural sensitivity, although their efforts were awkward on many occasions. Their sincere attempts (feeble as they were) stand in stark contrast to later interactions between Natives of the American West and European colonists that ended tragically for the Indians. Each tribe, like all cultures, had some elements that were good, some evil, but most were morally neutral. None of the tribes, nor the expedition itself, can be held up as an ideal. Each person is fallen and subject to sin, yet created in God's image. The expedition's experience in cultural diversity is useful to our parable of project leadership because much of the Heroic Venture has to do with dealing with people and situations that are new and unfamiliar.

The final reason for highlighting the Corps of Discovery is the huge amount of detail recorded in their journals. Their abundant narrative provides colorful illustrations for the important biblical principles of project leadership. There are few voyages into the unknown that have more recorded specifics than the Lewis and Clark Expedition. President Teddy Roosevelt said about Lewis and Clark's journals, "few explorers who saw and did so much that was absolutely new have written their deeds with such quiet absence of boastfulness and have drawn their descriptions with such complete freedom from exaggeration."[1]

The chapters of this book follow the chronological narrative of the Lewis and Clark Expedition. The opening section of each chapter summarizes the expedition's events, and is followed by discussion of Bible stories illustrating principles of project leadership. At the end of the narrative there is a references section that provides practical tools to help you with your specific vision. May these references give you concrete ways to fan into flame the passion burning within you.

I am deeply grateful for Stephen Ambrose's portrayal of the Lewis and Clark Expedition, entitled *Undaunted Courage* (New York: Simon and Schuster, 1996). This remarkable telling of their story provided me with the historical evidences I used to write *The Heroic Venture*. While there are many excellent accounts of the Lewis and Clark story, I highly recommend *Undaunted Courage* for anyone who wants to learn more about the details of this amazing journey.

Intimacy With Christ

The content of *The Heroic Venture* focuses on what we "do" in ministry. There is no attention given to the importance of "being" God's person. My assumption is that you are firmly committed to the biblical principle of "being" God's person before "doing" God's work. No amount of passion or wisdom can replace the importance of growing in Christlike character and being committed to the authority of God's Word. You will be effective in ministry only if you are growing in an intimate relationship with Christ, bearing fruit in godly character.

The fear of the Lord is the beginning of wisdom,
and the knowledge of the Holy One is insight.
~ Proverbs 9.10

Notes

[1] Ambrose, Stephen. 1996. *Undaunted Courage.* New York: Simon and Schuster, page 109.

Section I: Beginning the Adventure

"*Entertaining as I do, the most confident hope of succeeding in a voyage which had formed a darling project of mine for the last ten years, I could but esteem this moment of my departure as among the most happy of my life.*"

~ Meriwether Lewis

Compelling Context

See now, I dwell in a house of cedar,
but the ark of God dwells in a tent. ~ *2 Samuel 7.2*

1492-1802

The Lewis and Clark Expedition was an epic journey that rivals the greatest ventures of world history. It is a classic story of courage, danger, suffering, unexpected turns of events, and intense resolve to accomplish a burning vision. It was one of the greatest projects of all time.

The expedition was set in the context of international politics, undercover spies, secret missions, and the prospect of unprecedented new business opportunities. It was also an exploration into one of the earth's final uncharted frontiers.

The expedition was triggered by a famous real estate transaction called *The Louisiana Purchase*. European colonization in North America was over three hundred years old and colonial governments were starting to consolidate their activities in the New World. Over the past centuries the French, English, Spanish, Portuguese, and Dutch had sent colonists and traders to claim and exploit the riches of the Americas. By 1800, the Dutch and Portuguese were minor players, Spain was a fading influence, and the French emperor, Napoleon Bonaparte, was engaging in costly wars that left him in desperate need of cash.

France had claim to the Louisiana territory that ran from the Mississippi River to what is now modern-day Montana, an area covering 15 states of the current United States. Napoleon knew that France was powerless to defend such a large area of land with her armies stretched so thin in other European wars.

Thomas Jefferson, the newly elected president of the United States, understood Napoleon's dilemma. Having recently served as ambassador to France, Jefferson was well aware of Napoleon's need for money and the impossibility of defending the French claim to Louisiana. So in 1802, Jefferson began negotiations that ended in 1803 with a massive land purchase for a mere $15,000,000.

In 1802, water travel was the primary means of transportation. Although there were more gadgets, weapons, and knowledge than the Greeks or Romans could have imagined two thousand years before, there had been virtually no improvement in the speed of moving goods. Nothing moved faster than a horse, and as far as the people of 1802 were concerned, nothing would ever go faster than a horse. There were only four roads that crossed to the western frontier, and road conditions were terrible. It took 6-8 weeks to move items from the Atlantic Ocean to the Mississippi River.

Ever since settlers arrived in the New World, the dream had been to find a water route to move goods from the Atlantic to the Pacific. Centuries of exploration had uncovered the best waterway connections from the Atlantic ocean to the Mississippi River, but in between the Mississippi and the Pacific was a huge expanse of unknown territory. No one knew exactly how wide the area was, what the people who lived there were like, what new wildlife existed, what plants grew there, or what the landscape was like. Even the Indian tribes who lived in local regions did not know how one area connected to another.

Several attempts were made during the last half of the 1700's to explore this region for the purpose of establishing trade with the Indians and opening a direct trade route to Asia without going around the horn of South America. In 1756, an exploration party was formed but never launched due to the outbreak of the French and Indian War. Four other expeditions were attempted after 1776, three of which were instigated by scientist/philosopher Thomas Jefferson.

These early expeditions were poorly planned, primarily because there were too many unknowns. It was impossible to know how many provisions to take without knowledge of the continent's size and terrain. The Western Continent proved much easier to speculate about than it was to explore.

In1789, British explorer Alexander Mackenzie found a reasonable Canadian route from Montreal to the Pacific through low-lying mountains, about four hundred miles north of the Louisiana Territory. This news brought new hope to all who dreamed of a water route to the Pacific. The passage might be both open and easy. The news of this British discovery threw Jefferson into manic activity. It could be said that Mackenzie's Canadian discovery gave birth to the Lewis and Clark Expedition.

In 1792, there was more good news. Robert Gray sailed from the Pacific into the Columbia River (modern day Portland, Oregon) and mapped it, providing useful information about the geography. Gray's expedition made the width of the Continent less of an unknown. Jefferson's desire for an all-water route across the continent, including reports on its soil, rivers, mountains, animals, plants, and Indian tribes, was intensifying.

In 1793, the American Philosophical Society (of which Jefferson had been a key leader for decades) offered $1,000 to any explorer who could make it to the Pacific and back. A small expedition was planned that would not raise the suspicions of the French, Spanish, or Indian tribes. A number of men volunteered to lead the party, and a French botanist was chosen, but he turned out to be a spy who was raising an army to attack the Spanish. It was another failed attempt.

By 1802, Jefferson was not only President of the United States, but also among the most knowledgeable people in the world in many scientific areas, with a hunger for more knowledge about the world. He believed the Blue Ridge mountains of Virginia might be the highest in North America. This assumption led him to believe that all the great western rivers came from a single, low-lying height of land. His logic was that the Mississippi River connected to the Missouri River, and that the Missouri originated from these mountains. This would mean that a short, easy portage across this western mountain range would connect with the Columbia River on the other side, thereby linking the Atlantic with the Pacific. By 1803, with the purchase of the Louisiana Territory, Jefferson now had an open door to freely explore the northwest water passage without fear of French resistance.

Jefferson believed the western Indian tribes were noble and that mutually beneficial trading relationships could be developed for peaceful co-existence with his nation's citizens. He was racing against the English settlements that were expanding south from Canada. Jefferson hoped to cement strong relationships with the native tribes before the British could get to them.

A great contest was on between two world superpowers. They did not trust each other, and were in an all-out competition for the greatest business prize of the century.

Birthplace of Passion

THE EVENTS of Jefferson's day compelled him to action. It is impossible to appreciate the importance of the Lewis and Clark Expedition without understanding the historical context from which it came. The circumstances of a situation drive people toward action, and a clear understanding of the context is what keeps passion alive in the face of obstacles. Context is the birthplace of passion.

When God's people see suffering, an unmet need, or an injustice, it spurs them to take action. Context provides the motivation behind the action. The Bible gives many good

examples where people were motivated by the context of
their situation.

Facing Extinction

After the conquest of the Promised Land, God called a
series of Judges to protect Israel from her surrounding
enemies. During this time, Israel went back and forth
between stages of obedience and rebellion, and experienced
varying states of foreign oppression. Deborah was a
prophetess under Canaanite opposition. Gideon battled
the Midianites. Jephthah was recruited under the threat of
the invading Ammonites, and Samson was assigned to
protect Israel from the Philistines. The threat of Israel's
extinction motivated these Judges to action.

Discontent

David had been king of Israel for a number of years, and
had just settled down in his Jerusalem palace. Meanwhile
the ark of the covenant resided in a distant town, housed in
a simple structure. David was not satisfied with the ark of
God being in such an obscure place. One day, he said to the
prophet Nathan, "See now, I dwell in a house of cedar, but
the ark of God dwells in a tent" (2 Sam. 7.2). David's
discontent with the present situation was driving him to
launch an important project. Nathan responded by saying,
"Go, do all that is in your heart, for the Lord is with you"
(2 Sam. 7.3).

Surviving Exile

The temple had been destroyed by Nebuchadnezzar and the temple articles made of gold had been taken hundreds of miles to Babylon, along with the Jewish people. In the seventieth year of exile, Zerubbabel was one of thousands of Jewish people still living far from their homeland. King Cyrus became king of Persia and announced his intention to release a group of exiles back to their native Israel, including Zerubbabel.

About fifty years later, during Israel's exile, Esther was a Jewish orphan being cared for by her Uncle Mordecai. The Persian prime minister, Haman, hated the Jews, especially Mordecai, who would not bow down to Haman. Haman was plotting to wipe out the Jews. At the same time, the wife of King Xerxes, Queen Vashti, was deposed and a new queen needed to be found. After a thorough search of all the land, Esther was chosen and became Xerxes' queen. Queen Esther and Prime Minister Haman were headed for a showdown.

Nehemiah was another Jewish exile, serving as cupbearer to a later king named Artaxerxes. Nehemiah received news that his native Jerusalem was in a shambles. He was told, "The remnant there in the province who had survived the exile is in great trouble and shame. The wall of Jerusalem is broken down, and its gates are destroyed by fire" (Neh. 1.3). Nehemiah was devastated. He wept, mourned, and fasted, and prayed for many days. The circumstances motivated him to action.

Messiah's Victory over Satan

Mankind was under the curse of sin and the domination of Satan. The world was in need of a Savior. The people were like a sheep without a shepherd. For centuries, God had prepared the Jewish people to be the culture from which Messiah would come. His coming had been promised and foretold many times throughout their history. The woman at the well expressed it best: "I know that Messiah is coming (he who is called Christ). When he comes, he will tell us all things" (John 4.25).

In this cosmic context was an ordinary young woman named Mary. She lived in a small, insignificant Jewish town called Nazareth, and was engaged to be married to a man named Joseph. An angel visited Mary to tell her some stunning news about God's design for her, and Joseph was informed of God's plan through a dream. If they agreed to God's will, their lives would be radically changed forever.

God recognized the appropriate context to send the Son to "deliver us from the domain of darkness" (Col. 1.13). It was the right time in human history, at the right geographic place in the world, for Jesus "to destroy the works of the devil" (1 John 3.8).

> *But when the fullness of time had come,*
> *God sent forth his Son, born of woman, born under the law,*
> *to redeem those who were under the law,*
> *so that we might receive adoption as sons.*
> *~ Galatians 4.4-5*

In all these examples it was the context that compelled the people to the task that followed. It was their circumstances that kept them pushing ahead, overcoming all odds. It is hard to imagine Nehemiah, Esther, David, Mary, or Zerubbabel losing sight of the events that brought them to their assignment. Passion comes from the pressing needs of the current situation.

The Compelling Context drives people to the Heroic Venture.

Questions for Discussion

1. What does it mean to say, "Context is the birthplace of passion?"
2. In this chapter, which Bible story relates the most to your present situation?
3. Think about your ministry today. What is the context that you find yourself in? What is the background story? What happened before you came into this situation?
4. What is unique to your life story that God might use for his glory in this situation?
5. What excites you about your context? What frustrates you? What motivates you? What other emotions do you have when you think about your context?

Burning Vision

If it pleases the king, and if your servant has found favor in your sight, that you send me to Judah, to the city of my fathers' graves, that I may rebuild it. ~ Nehemiah 2.5

1802

Centuries of exploration, scientific advancement, colonization, and business development created the backdrop for Thomas Jefferson to clearly articulate his vision:

> **Find the most direct all-water route from the Mississippi to the Pacific Ocean across the western two-thirds of the continent and return safely with scientific information about the land.**

All the pieces were in place:

⋄ *Jefferson had the influence he needed as newly elected President of the United States. He was no longer simply a prominent member of the American Philosophical Society and high-ranking government official, but one of the most powerful people in the world.*

⋄ *With the Louisiana Purchase, Jefferson did not have to be concerned about French resistance to an expedition.*

❖ *Recent discoveries were eliminating some of the previous "unknowns" that made previous expeditions unsuccessful.*

❖ *Jefferson believed that a good relationship could be formed with the Indian tribes and that he could provide a more attractive alliance than the British.*

❖ *The English were closing fast on finding the water passage and in solidifying friendship with the Indian tribes.*

Time was of the essence. It was the right moment for an expedition.

EVENTS CONVERGED in such a way that it became obvious that the time was right for Jefferson's dream to become reality. In the same way, God uses circumstances to give his people a Burning Vision to do his work.

Someone Needs to Do Something!

When God's people recognize the context of the needs around them, the inevitable result is a desire to meet those needs. When Christians see a problem, they start saying, "Someone needs to do something!" When men and women start to imagine specific ways to deal with the problem, the result is a Burning Vision.

Vision is the most important part of ministry projects. Vision is what defines the specific task. Every project in biblical history involved a clear vision.

Sometimes God gives specific direction on what needs to be done. Other times people develop a vision out of their own passion and God blesses it (see Reference H, at the back of this book, for a list of thirty projects in the Bible and the origin of their vision).

Specific Direction

Noah was a righteous man living in the midst of a world of great evil.

> The Lord saw that the wickedness of man was great in the earth, and that every intention of the thoughts of his heart was only evil continually. And the Lord was sorry that he had made man on the earth, and it grieved him to his heart.
>
> Genesis 6.5-6

In response to the wickedness of the day, God instructed Noah to build an ark of specific dimensions that would provide safety for his family and the animals of the earth.

Abraham was from Ur, part of modern-day Iraq. He was a believer in God, but lived in a land of idolatry. He was seventy-five years old when he was directed to leave the luxury and familiar surroundings of his home and travel to Canaan, a distant and unknown land.

Abraham was told he would be made into a great nation, a blessing to all nations, even though he was an old man and without children. Abraham's assignment began a new and important phase of God's plan to defeat the devil by sending Jesus through the line of Abraham.

Moses was asked to lead more than a million Jewish slaves out of Egyptian bondage. Moses not only had to convince Pharaoh to release this wealth of free labor, but he also had to transform a slave nation into the culture that would nurture and receive the Messiah. It was a daunting task. Other significant projects given to Moses included the construction the tabernacle, conducting a census of the people (twice), and sending out a contingent of twelve spies to investigate the Promised Land.

Many others received a Burning Vision specifically from God:

◇ *Jonah was sent to tell the Ninevites that their city would be overturned in forty days.*

◇ *Mary and Joseph were given the awesome responsibility of raising the Messiah, even relocating the family to Egypt for a period of time.*

◇ *Jesus sent the seventy-two disciples to preach the Good News (Luke 10.1-17).*

◇ *Peter was sent to preach to Cornelius.*

❖ *Paul and Barnabas were specifically set apart by the Holy Spirit to take the Gospel to the Gentiles. For the rest of his life, this was a Burning Vision that Paul would never take lightly.*

Their Own Initiative

David, out of his own initiative and desire to see the ark housed in a more suitable location, had a vision to build a temple to honor the Lord. Solomon received David's plans and finished the construction. Years later, King Jehoash noticed that the temple was in need of repair and ordered a remodeling project. King Hezekiah organized a national Passover celebration after purifying that same temple.

During Israel's captivity, Esther and Mordecai, under the threat of Jewish extinction, urgently developed a strategy to prevent Jewish genocide, using Esther's influence as queen of Persia. A few years later, King Cyrus, in response to a prophetic word, ordered the rebuilding of the temple and the release of several temple articles. Several Levite priests were eager to take on the project, including Zerubbabel.

Nehemiah was grieved over the disgrace of Jerusalem's burned and broken wall and desired to rebuild it. As cupbearer, he had access to the king, but he waited four months for the right moment. God provided the opportunity when Nehemiah's grief began to show on his face. (He had never expressed sadness in the king's presence, a capital offense in that culture.) When the king asked Nehemiah's request, Nehemiah was ready with a straightforward reply: "Send me to Judah, to the city of my fathers' graves, that I may rebuild it" (Neh. 2.5).

How God Leads

God leads men and women toward a Burning Vision in a variety of ways. (For more discussion, see Reference E, *Discerning God's Will*.)

◇ *Abraham and Peter received a vision.*

◇ *Joseph (Jacob's son) and Joseph (Jesus' father) heard from God in a dream.*

◇ *Joshua, Gideon, Samson (through his parents), Mary, and Philip were visited by angels.*

◇ *Barak, Zerubbabel, Paul, and Barnabas received a prophetic word.*

◇ *Jephthah and Esther were instructed by their leaders.*

◇ *David, Hezekiah, Jehoash, and Nehemiah carried out their projects on their own initiative, out of their own heart's passion for God.*

◇ *The apostles, and the group of seventy-two, were specifically commissioned by Christ himself.*

The Greatest Assignment

The Great Commission (Matt. 28.18-20) is the greatest project ever given to mankind. The apostles, and the rest of the Church at large, are given the overarching mission of making disciples of all nations, "and then the end will come" (Matt. 24.14). Under this grand vision, the Holy Spirit leads people into specific projects to support his plan. God ignites passion in his people as they see ways to meet needs locally and throughout the world. The Burning Vision that results in specific ministries is how God accomplishes his work. God still leads people into a Heroic Venture.

Questions for Discussion

1. Do you have the beginnings of a Burning Vision that you cannot get out of your mind? Summarize it in a sentence or two. *Note: If you are concerned about your lack of passion, see Reference F, "What If I Have No Passion?"*
2. How did you receive this Burning Vision?
3. How have these thoughts and dreams developed over the weeks, months, or years?
4. How does your Burning Vision fit with God's purposes in the world?
5. With which biblical characters do you most relate as you consider your own Burning Vision?

Personal Calling

And who knows whether you have not come to the kingdom
for such a time as this? ~ Esther 4.14

1802

By 1802, Meriwether Lewis, in his late twenties, had become
the obvious choice to lead the expedition. Since 1801, when
Jefferson was elected President, Lewis had been serving as
Jefferson's presidential secretary, similar to what today would
be called the Chief of Staff.

Jefferson had been Lewis' close, personal mentor for many
years, covering a variety of scientific and political topics.
Jefferson knew Lewis as a man of "sound understanding and
a fidelity to truth." Jefferson had no question about Lewis'
loyalty or his abilities to take on the complex task required to
fulfill the vision. Under Jefferson's instruction, Lewis had become an accomplished scientist, sharing Jefferson's passion for
plants, animals, geography, languages, and cultures. In 1802,
Lewis was at Jefferson's home when the Mackenzie report,
describing the geography of northwest Canada, was delivered
to Jefferson. The two devoured it together with delight.

As a young man, Lewis served in the army, eventually becoming
paymaster. This responsibility required him to travel throughout

the western frontier to deliver pay to the soldiers. This is where he learned his frontier skills.

In 1793, Lewis was one of the eager volunteers who wanted to lead the western expedition that was eventually led by the French spy. Lewis was passed over because of his youth (he was only 18 years old), but his passion for the mission was noteworthy, and helped him land the job ten years later, when the time was right.

Lewis had a natural curiosity that would allow him to be trained in all the scientific skills he would be called upon to use. Enormous amounts of scientific information would have to be recorded about the people, wildlife, and geography he encountered. He would have to learn how to take measurements with which to construct a map, lead a group of men into an unknown territory, and return safely. It was a huge job with tremendous risks.

Jefferson observed in Lewis several instances of depression which he had also seen in Lewis' father. Although the bouts of depression did not rule Lewis out, they were a cause of concern about Lewis' ability to lead the mission. In addition, critics said Lewis was not well educated and too much of a risk taker.

Lewis did exhibit occasional lapses in judgment. For example, in 1803, when the expedition was waiting for supplies in St. Louis, Lewis proposed a side trip to Santa Fe, New Mexico, which was in Spanish territory. Lewis thought he could make good use of time instead of waiting around doing nothing. Jefferson was appalled. Such a distraction would imperil the mission by introducing the Spanish into the equation. Jefferson ended the discussion by firmly re-emphasizing Lewis' mission to find a direct water route formed by the Missouri River.

Jefferson was not blind to Lewis' shortcomings, which seemed to worsen when Lewis drank too much alcohol. However, few people had his credentials in botany, natural history, minerals, medicine, and astronomy, coupled with his firm constitution, leadership qualities, ability to learn quickly, knowledge of the western woods, and contact with Indian cultures. There was no doubt that Meriwether Lewis was Jefferson's man for the job.

MERIWETHER LEWIS had many weaknesses, and his critics were vocal about pointing them out. Yet Jefferson was certain that Lewis was the person to represent him. In the same way, God chooses men and women to represent him, despite the constant accusations made by the enemy. God has used, and will use, imperfect people to carry out his plans.

A Variety of Imperfections
Once the vision is defined, the right leader is needed to carry out the task.

God calls people to carry out his work. He calls men and women from varied backgrounds, ages, and occupations. Looking at the examples in the Bible, there is no single profile. They were old and young, experienced and neo-phyte, arrogant and unsure, proven leaders and beginners. The leaders God chose were as diverse as could be.

They were also far from perfect:

⋄ *Noah got drunk at the end of his mission.*

⋄ *Abraham lied to save his life.*

⋄ *Joseph was arrogant.*

⋄ *Moses balked at his assignment and had to have Aaron as a spokesman.*

⋄ *Barak insisted on Deborah's help in defeating the Canaanites.*

⋄ *Gideon was a "nobody," threshing wheat, who needed four different confirmations to ease his doubts before he believed God.*

⋄ *Samson was undisciplined, controlled by sensuality, and confided in untrustworthy people.*

⋄ *Jephthah was an illegitimate son of a prostitute, who made a rash vow.*

⋄ *David was infamous for his adultery and murder.*

⋄ *Solomon fell into idolatry.*

❖ *Hezekiah's heart was proud, not responding to the kindness God showed him.*

❖ *Jonah took a ship in the opposite direction from his assigned destination, going as far away as he could get.*

❖ *Peter denied the Lord.*

❖ *Paul killed Christians.*

❖ *The apostles were rough, uneducated men.*

Just about every vice known to mankind is exhibited in these representatives of God's tasks. Yet despite their imperfections, God worked through them. This gives hope that he can use anyone to do his work.

Excuses

Sometimes, when people get a vision, they want someone else to carry it out. Like Moses at the burning bush, they want to make excuses, such as:

❖ *"I am too old" (Abraham started out old).*

❖ *"I am too young" (Mary was probably a teenager when she was called).*

❖ *"I do not have the right education or background" (Peter was a fisherman who had less education than most modern fourth-grade children).*

41

⋄ *"I am not the right race or culture"* (*Jonah was very different from the people of Nineveh whom he led to repentance*).

⋄ *"I am not from the right family"* (*Gideon was from the least family from the least tribe in Israel*).

God's Advance Work

God was already at work in the lives of his people when their assignments emerged.

⋄ *Moses had world-class training in the court of Pharaoh, and also knew the "backwoods" of the desert through which he would lead the Israelites out of slavery.*

⋄ *David's years as a shepherd exposed him to protecting the sheep and defeating fierce prey, helping him become a mighty warrior. Years of solitude made him a reflective "man after God's own heart" (1 Sam. 13.14).*

⋄ *Nehemiah, as cupbearer to the king, had access to the king of Persia and all his resources when it was time to rebuild the wall.*

⋄ *The seventy-two disciples watched Jesus minister before they were sent out by twos to preach the Good News.*

⋄ *Paul's training as a Pharisee served him well in debating the Judaizers and other heretical teachers.*

God especially prepared Esther for her task. Among the beautiful women of King Xerxes' time, Esther was in Persian captivity when she was selected as queen to replace the deposed Queen Vashti. Esther was in the palace only a short time when she received shocking news from her guardian, Mordecai. The king's top official, Haman, was about to exterminate all the Jews living in the land. Mordecai urged Esther to beg the king's mercy on their behalf.

Esther explained that it was not as simple as it seemed to get an audience with the king, even in her queenly capacity. The king could summon others, but no one initiated contact with the king upon penalty of death. It had been thirty days since Esther had been called in. Mordecai pressed Esther, saying:

> Do not think to yourself that in the king's palace you will escape any more than all the other Jews. For if you keep silent at this time, relief and deliverance will rise for the Jews from another place, but you and your father's house will perish. And who knows whether you have not come to the kingdom for such a time as this?
>
> ~ Esther 4.13-14

Confirmation

Just as God prepares people for their calling, he also confirms his calling through miraculous signs, or the testimony of others. God used the prophecy of Jeremiah to lead King Cyrus to authorize the rebuilding of the temple. Cyrus' release of the temple's treasures, stolen away to Babylon decades earlier, was further confirmation of God's hand.

When Mary visited Elizabeth, who did not know of Mary's pregnancy, Elizabeth proclaimed God's confirmation, saying:

> Blessed are you among women, and blessed is the fruit of your womb! And why is this granted to me that the mother of my Lord should come to me? For behold, when the sound of your greeting came to my ears, the baby in my womb leaped for joy. And blessed is she who believed that there would be a fulfillment of what was spoken to her from the Lord.
>
> ~ Luke 1.42-45

Like Them, You Can Do Great Things

By faith, the people of God accomplished great things. They:

> conquered kingdoms, enforced justice, obtained promises, stopped the mouths of lions, quenched the power of fire, escaped the edge of the sword, were made strong out of weakness, became mighty in war, put foreign armies to flight.
>
> ~ Hebrews 11.33-34

God still issues a Personal Calling to his people to complete the Heroic Venture for his glory.

Questions for Discussion

1. Look at the people God used to accomplish his purposes. What were their shortcomings?
2. Were their failures any greater than yours? If God could use them in mighty ways, is he still able to use you?
3. Which one of the biblical characters do you relate to the most? Why?
4. God was at work in the lives of his people, even before they were called to their Heroic Venture. Looking back, how was God at work in your life to prepare you for today?
5. Many of God's people made excuses when God gave them their assignment. Have you ever made excuses to God? If so, what are they? If not, have you noticed others making excuses?

Vital Preparations

And God sent me before you
to preserve for you a remnant on earth,
and to keep alive for you many survivors. ~ Genesis 45.7

Early 1803

Despite all of Meriwether Lewis' abilities, passions, interests, loyalties, and skills, he still needed to receive considerable training and make massive amounts of preparation before he was ready to lead the expedition.

With Jefferson as his tutor, Lewis had learned quite a bit. Jefferson had the world's most extensive library on North America. But Lewis still needed more specific instruction in botany, geography, minerals, astronomy, and ethnology, so in 1803, Lewis went to Philadelphia for crash courses from the leading thinkers of the day.

While he was studying, Lewis also needed to prepare for the journey. In a sea of uncertainty, some things were known. Accurate maps had been made from the connection of the Missouri and Mississippi (near today's St. Louis) to the Mandan villages (in current-day Bismark, North Dakota). The Columbia River had also been charted inland from the Pacific Ocean through today's Portland, Oregon. There were wild guesses and speculation about what was in between. Accurate celestial measurements needed to be taken at points along the trip so an accurate map could be made. Training in taking astronomical measurements and map making was especially important.

In this mass of uncertainty, the planning process needed to take place. Supplies had to be procured, a team assembled, and a timetable predicted. They would be out of supply range for an unknown period of time. Forecasting the amount of provisions was especially difficult when the plant and animal life was unknowable. If they brought enough ammunition, could they live off the land? What kind of medicine might they need with strange animals or reptiles lurking about? How many men were needed and with what skills? How big a boat? What design? What type of rifles? How much powder and lead? How many cooking pots? What tools? How much rations could be carried? What scientific instruments and books to bring? How many fishing hooks? Details! Details!

In terms of the Indians they might meet along the way, Jefferson's orders were clear: "In all your intercourse with natives treat them in the most friendly and conciliatory manner which their own conduct will admit. Invite the chiefs to come to Washington to meet with me."

The rumor was that the Indians between St. Louis and the Mandan village were hostile and well armed. They had a reputation for demanding ransom for safe passage along the Missouri River. There were many legends about the western Indian tribes, especially the Sioux. Some speculated they were the lost tribe of Israel or a wandering tribe of Welshman. Such wide speculation created a new set of questions. How could they introduce friendly relations if the first tribes they encountered turned out to be hostile? What kind of presents would be welcomed by the Indian tribes of which they knew nothing?

It was an overwhelming task to answer all the questions, procure what was needed, all while attending intensive studies in every scientific area known to Americans in 1803.

The initial plan was to leave St. Louis on August 1, 1803 with a party of twelve men, spend the winter in the Mandan Indian village, cross the mountains to the Pacific and return to St. Louis before the winter of 1804 set in.

One of the primary jobs Lewis had was overseeing the design and construction of a special modular iron boat for the journey down the Columbia River. Lewis loved the boat but had trouble building it. He spent inordinate amounts of time on it at Harpers Ferry, Virginia, before going to Philadelphia for his education, much to the dismay of Jefferson. Jefferson feared Lewis would miss the August 1 deadline by spending so much time on this pet project.

Jefferson's concerns about the schedule were realized. By the time the boat was assembled and Lewis' education completed, it was clear the expedition would not be ready to leave by August 1803 and would have to wait until the spring of 1804.

ALL PROJECTS require attention to detail and careful preparation. The Lewis and Clark Expedition was among the more complicated projects in history, but even the simplest project requires preparation.

Personal Preparation

Once people are called to start a ministry, despite the advance work of God, there are often additional aspects of preparation before launching the Heroic Venture.

In some cases, additional biblical or ministry training may be needed. The Urban Ministry Institute (see Reference J) is an excellent source of training for ministry.

Some people need to serve under an experienced person before taking the mantle of leadership. For example, God placed Joshua under Moses' leadership to prepare him for the future.

After Paul's conversion, he went through many years of training and instruction before God sent him out as a missionary with Barnabas (Acts 13). One noteworthy project Paul and Barnabas carried out together was the collection of an offering to help the suffering Jerusalem church (Acts 11.27-30). This must have been an instructive project that prepared Paul and Barnabas to be an effective missionary band.

In the same way, Jesus "grew and became strong, filled with wisdom. And the favor of God was upon him" (Luke

2.40) and he "increased in wisdom and in stature and in favor with God and man" (Luke 2.52). He went through many years of preparation in his parents' household before his time for public ministry had come.

Logistics and Details

Besides training, there are often logistical details to consider. Even before the king knew what was on Nehemiah's mind, Nehemiah had done his homework, figuring what supplies and logistical support would be needed to rebuild the wall. When the king asked Nehemiah what he wanted, Nehemiah was prepared, saying:

> If it pleases the king, let letters be given me to the governors of the province Beyond the River, that they may let me pass through until I come to Judah, and a letter to Asaph, the keeper of the king's forest, that he may give me timber to make beams for the gates of the fortress of the temple, and for the wall of the city, and for the house that I shall occupy.
> ~ Nehemiah 2.7-8

Moses received precise details from God about how the tabernacle was to be constructed and which craftsman was assigned to each task. In chapter after chapter of Exodus 25-31, God tells Moses what materials are needed, how to gather them, and what each part should look like.

Joshua was given a specific set of instructions for the people to follow in order to ensure the fall of Jericho. They were asked to march around the city seven times each day for a week, and then to give a great shout, at which time the wall of Jericho would fall. God did the work, but it took Joshua and his leaders some effort to mobilize such a large group of people.

David was given a detailed vision by the Holy Spirit of the plans for the temple's construction. It included the portico, storerooms, treasuries, upper parts, inner rooms, outer courts, and the place of atonement. David gave Solomon instructions on the division of labor for the priests and other workers, including how the services should be conducted. He was specific about the details of the lampstands, tables, dishes, and the altar, including the weights of silver and gold in each article. David said, "All this he made clear to me in writing from the hand of the Lord, all the work to be done according to the plan" (1 Chron. 28.19).

Esther, when admonished by Mordecai to intercede on behalf of the Jews, set in motion specific preparations:

> Go, gather all the Jews to be found in Susa, and hold a fast on my behalf, and do not eat or drink for three days, night or day. I and my young women will also fast as you do. Then I will go to the king, though it is against the law.
>
> ~ Esther 4.16

Prayer is always a Vital Preparation.

Before Zerubbabel began rebuilding the temple, he helped the people settle in their towns after their seventy-year exile. Then he and his fellow priests started building the altar so the people could begin worshiping. With these important preparations in place, the temple could be built with great resolve.

God's Preparation for Joseph

Joseph's entire life-purpose was to provide a way of salvation for his people. Joseph received personal experience in management skills running Potiphar's household, but he was also gifted by God in the area of logistical details.

When summoned to interpret Pharaoh's dream, the king's officials were amazed not only by Joseph's ability to predict the future, but at his wise strategy to deal with the calamity. Joseph proposed storing of grain that could be kept in reserve during the lean years, "so that the land may not perish through the famine" (Gen. 41.36). Pharaoh was so impressed that he said, "Can we find a man like this, in whom is the Spirit of God?" (41.38).

Joseph recognized, many years later, that God had prepared him for this task. He confessed to his brothers, "And God sent me before you to preserve for you a remnant on earth, and to keep alive for you many survivors" (Gen. 45.7).

As God prepares his people through previous experiences, project leaders must be willing to do the hard work of tending to the Vital Preparations before pursuing the Heroic Venture.[1]

Questions for Discussion

1. How has God prepared you for your present ministry?
2. In the projects in the Bible, explain when logistics and details were important to accomplish the vision.
3. Why do you think God had his people go through so much work and preparation to achieve his purposes? For example, why not simply create the temple instead of having David and Solomon take all those years to build it?
4. When do you find yourself tempted to skip over the Vital Preparations needed to see vision come to reality? What are the areas you are tempted to skip over?
5. What further training or preparation do you need to make you more effective?

Notes

[1] For practical help in addressing the Vital Preparations of your ministry, see the following references:

Reference C - *Projects: The Outlet for Ministry Passion*
Reference D - *How to Implement Your Ministry Vision*
Reference G - *Vision versus Goals: How Are They Different?*

Committed Team

*Set apart for me Barnabas and Saul for the work
to which I have called them.* ~ Acts 13.2

1803 - May 1804

In 1803, as Lewis considered his plans, he realized the need for
a second officer. If Lewis died, another officer could bring back
the journals and discoveries. A second officer could also en-
force discipline. Lewis immediately thought of his old army
commander, William Clark. Clark was tough woodsman
accustomed to command, a good waterman and surveyor,
and an excellent map maker. The inclusion of Clark would yield
an additional benefit. Clark would bring his trusted African-
American slave, York, to join the expedition. York's experience,
talents, and bravery would contribute to the mission's success.

Where Lewis was shaky, Clark was strong and vice versa. Both
were competent for the task, reliable, and effective leaders of
men. While divided command almost never works in the
military (disagreeing commanders can result in death to the
unit), Lewis trusted that it could work with Clark.

Although they would share joint command, each would have
specific roles. Clark would manage the boat and take map
readings. Lewis would walk along the shore to collect data and
specimens. Lewis also appointed himself the doctor, since he

studied under the famous physician of the day, Benjamin Rush. Lewis knew how to set broken bones, deal with dysentery and croup, and was familiar with the use of wild herbs for treating various ailments. Lewis would have a few medical supplies, but would have to improvise, using what was available in nature along the way.

With the command structure in place, Lewis set out to build the rest of the team. He needed twelve healthy military men of good character, who were proficient hunters. The success of the enterprise would depend on careful selection of capable and compatible men. A long journey into the wilderness, full of unknowns, would be difficult if the team was not committed to the vision. On July 4, 1803, the Louisiana Purchase was announced to the public, which greatly increased national interest in the expedition. The word about recruitment got out on the western frontier, so Lewis and Clark could be highly selective.

Lewis was given authorization to hire non-military guides and interpreters that could contribute to the expedition's success, but they needed to share the soldier's hardiness and character. One such non-military member was George Drouillard, a frontier hunter-trapper and scout. He was proficient in Indian cultures and languages, knew French and sign language, and had a calm confidence about him that made him a welcome member of the expedition.

In November, 1803, the developing team departed St. Louis on the Mississippi River toward the confluence of the Missouri River at St. Charles, where they would begin their expedition the following Spring. The power of the Mississippi awed them. It became clear they would need a bigger team. Much more muscle was needed. More specific roles had to be assigned, such as one person to watch for trees and changing currents. As a result, they doubled the size of the team.

More men meant more supplies and new planning. New authorization was needed from the President to spend more money. They had to reorganize and get adequate supplies. This was no small task in 1803 when it took six to eight weeks to transport supplies from the east, and many weeks for mail to travel back and forth.

The team had been stationed in St. Charles for four months and had very little to keep them occupied. They were young men in great physical shape, waiting around to start their adventure, so they fought, drank, and were sometimes insubordinate. They knew this expedition would be the high point of their lives–if they survived. They were confident and eager to make history. But they were forced to wait for ample supplies.

As the launch date approached, a ceremony was held to enlist the twenty-five members of the Corps of Discovery, who were "destined for the expedition through the interior of the Continent of North America." Another five members would go to Mandan winter quarters and return with reports and specimens. They were divided into three squads with a sergeant overseeing each one.

A troubling mixup emerged when Clark's commission was issued below the promised rank of captain. Lewis was furious, but Clark was willing to overlook the insult for the sake of the expedition. The men were never told; as far as they knew, both Lewis and Clark were the captains.

Finally, on May 14, 1804, the party left St. Charles with joyful spirits. Their Heroic Venture up the Missouri River had begun. They were leaving connection with the outside world. There would be no orders, commissions, fresh supplies, or reinforcements. They expected to be gone for two years. There would be no more guidance from superiors. Lewis and Clark were given an independent military command, the likes of which had never been given before or since.

Out on the river, they faced a steady current as they experienced a variety of islands, sandbars, and narrow channels. Uprooted trees that had fallen into the river often had to be pushed out of the way, along with branches and limbs that threatened to poke holes in the boat. It was even more treacherous than the Mississippi.

Their keel boat was an ungainly craft with cargo aboard and going upstream was almost impossible. Unless there was a wind they had to push and pull boat upriver. At times they had to rush from one side of the boat to another to keep it from toppling over. Conditions required everyone aboard to be tough, quick, and alert. Thanks to the exertion of the men, the boat and its contents were saved from overturning on countless occasions. They were always ready to make any effort required for the sake of the enterprise.

The Corps met up with a Frenchman who knew Clark's brother and understood the Yankton Sioux language. One of the expedition's goals was to send one of the Sioux chiefs to visit Jefferson back in Washington D.C., and they would need a guide to accomplish this goal. So they persuaded the French-man to join the party as an escort back to the nation's capitol.

Some of the team members were assigned to daily hunting duty. Sergeants were given command over various parts of the boat. Privates under their command handled steering, baggage, compass, sails, oars, and lookout. Others were assigned to ward off floating debris, or call out warnings of dangers ahead, such as sandbars or whirlpools.

They were beginning to understand how to operate as a team.

LEWIS AND CLARK showed their leadership ability by assigning specific roles to talented people. Each person made a unique contribution to the overall enterprise. Lewis and Clark shared joint command of the operation, each using his own respective strengths. Collaboration like that required unselfishness, and a firm belief in the strength of others to compensate for their own weaknesses.

Most great projects involve a team of people committed to the vision. Teams give a project the strength of diverse talents, experiences, and mutual encouragement. As a team, tasks can be completed in much less time and with far less effort than they can individually. In ministry, leaders need to believe in other team members because they have spiritual gifts that the leader lacks. A project leader can collaborate with confidence because the Holy Spirit can be trusted to be at work in others.

The Power of Team

Moses and Aaron served together, sharing the load of responsibility. God used Aaron as a confirmation of Moses' call. At the burning bush, God told Moses that Aaron was already on the way to meet Moses. God often confirms his call through others.

God also instructed Moses to use a team of twelve spies to scout the Promised Land, with one representative from each tribe. Moses utilized tribal representation on two other occasions when God commanded him to take a census of the people.

Esther and Mordecai worked together as a team. Esther was in the position of power but was humble enough to listen to Mordecai's advice. She could have proudly exercised her authority as queen, but remained teachable to his wise counsel. Mordecai trusted Esther to follow through with wisdom and courage.

When King Cyrus sent the exiles back to rebuild the temple, Zerubbabel was one of many team members to undertake the project. When the Israelites had settled in their towns the people assembled as one man in Jerusalem. Then Jeshua, son of Jozadak, and his fellow priests and Zerubbabel, son of Shealtiel, and his associates began to build the altar of God (Ezra 3.1, 2).

They split up the duties among those who were skilled in various crafts. "So they gave money to the masons and the carpenters, and food, drink, and oil to the Sidonians and the Tyrians to bring cedar trees from Lebanon to the sea, to Joppa" (Ezra 3.7).

Some get a vision for a project and discover it is God's will for others to finish it. Such was the case with David and the temple. It was in David's heart to build a place for the ark to dwell; a place to honor the Lord. But it was his son, Solomon, who actually completed the job. Sometimes a team involves people who take different phases to reach the project's completion.

During his missionary journeys, the Apostle Paul continually showed his commitment to team ministry by forming apostolic bands to accompany him. Paul and Barnabas joined as the first of these teams when the church at Antioch laid hands on them. By prophetic word, God said, "Set apart for me Barnabas and Saul for the work to which I have called them" (Acts 13.2). Paul had many other teammates including Luke, Silas, Timothy, Erastus,

Sopater, Aristarchus, Secundus, Gaius, Tychicus, and Trophimus (Acts 20.4-5).

When it was time to send his seventy-two disciples out to do ministry, Jesus sent them in teams of two. He knew the power of shared experience, mutual encouragement, and mutual dependence.

Shared Commitment to Vision

Choosing the right people, who share the vision, is critical to the Heroic Venture. Clark showed his commitment to the vision when he overlooked the insult of not receiving the promised rank of captain. He had a right to complain and cause a scene, but he stayed quiet for the good of the expedition.

Zerubbabel showed wisdom by preventing people from joining the team when they did not share the vision.

> Now when the adversaries of Judah and Benjamin heard that the returned exiles were building a temple to the Lord, the God of Israel, they approached Zerubbabel and the heads of fathers' houses and said to them, "Let us build with you, for we worship your God as you do, and we have been sacrificing to him."
>
> ~ Ezra 4.1-2

Zerubbabel saw through their deception and took action.

But Zerubbabel, Jeshua, and the rest of the heads of fathers' houses in Israel said to them, "You have nothing to do with us in building a house to our God; but we alone will build to the Lord."

~ Ezra 4.3

A Gifted Team Builder

Nehemiah showed how to build a Committed Team. When Nehemiah first arrived in Jerusalem to rebuild the wall, he kept his mission a secret. After staying three days, he said, "Then I arose in the night, I and a few men with me. And I told no one what my God had put into my heart to do for Jerusalem" (Neh. 2.12). With these men accompanying him, he thoroughly examined the key parts of the wall which had been destroyed. Without spelling out his vision, he allowed the men to see the devastation in great detail. Then he said:

"You see the trouble we are in, how Jerusalem lies in ruins with its gates burned. Come, let us build the wall of Jerusalem, that we may no longer suffer derision." And I told them of the hand of my God that had been upon me for good, and also of the words that the king had spoken to me. And they said, "Let us rise up and build." So they strengthened their hands for the good work.

~ Nehemiah 2.17-18

Nehemiah's team was on board because of Nehemiah's presentation of the need, and the encouragement of God's supernatural provision through the king.

Nehemiah is also a great study in delegation and inspiration. He appointed a team of leaders to be in charge of various parts of the construction project. His skillful leadership resulted in completion of the work ahead of schedule while "the people worked with all their heart" (Neh. 4.6, NIV).

A gifted, Committed Team can make the task enjoyable. Team members, despite causing occasional aggravation, are a blessing, and vital to the Heroic Venture.

Questions for Discussion

1. How did Meriwether Lewis make use of teamwork?
2. What has been your experience of working on a team?
3. How do the gifts of the Holy Spirit make a difference in completing a project?
4. What are the drawbacks of having a team? When do you prefer working by yourself?
5. Why is it important to have a team in completing projects?

Section II: Triumph and Heartbreak

"I will cheerfully join you and partake of the dangers, difficulties, and fatigues and I anticipate the honors and rewards of the result of such an enterprise."

~ *William Clark's acceptance of Lewis' invitation*
to co-lead the expedition

I n t e r n a l   C o m p l i c a t i o n s

*All the people of Israel grumbled against Moses and Aaron.
The whole congregation said to them,
"Would that we had died in the land of Egypt!"* ~ Numbers 14.2

July - August 1804

By July 4, 1804, America's birthday, the expedition was entering
new terrain, rejoicing at the entry to a beautiful, open, extensive prairie. They discovered an unknown creek and named it
Independence Creek, in honor of their native country. The
beauty of the grass, hills, and valleys was overwhelming. They
were excited to start cataloging the new animals and plants,
unseen on the eastern continent, including the badger, prairie
dog, buffalo, antelope, jackrabbit, mule deer, elk, magpie, and
coyote. A special ration of whiskey and a shot from the cannon
helped the men celebrate Independence Day.

The men turned their attention to the dangers ahead. Always
on Lewis' mind were the Indian tribes along the Missouri and
beyond. Lewis knew that he carried an unprecedented arsenal
of weapons that might tempt native tribes. Any Indian nation in
possession of these weapons would dominate their region for
a long time to come. Although their weaponry was intimidating
enough to scare away smaller war parties, a large group could
easily overpower Lewis and Clark's men.

Lewis' hope was that the Indians would talk and trade rather than try to kill the party. He did not want a fight but he and Clark made sure they were never caught by surprise. A camp of sleeping men would be a great temptation, so they camped on islands whenever possible.

On August 2, they met with their first Indian tribe, the Otos. Lewis and Clark asked if a peace treaty could be brokered between the Otos and the Sioux. The Otos said it was possible, but it would cost the party some whiskey to make it happen. Although the Otos were not impressed with the tobacco, paint, and beads offered to them, the expedition's first Indian encounter had gone relatively well. In spite of these relatively successful events since their launch, the party would soon face many difficulties.

On August 18, one of the members, Moses Reed, deserted the party. When he was found, he was tried in a court martial, found guilty, beaten, and banished from the party. He was forced to give up his rifle and would be sent back to St. Louis with the group the next spring.

Another disciplinary problem emerged later, again involving Private Reed. He was a grousing malcontent who poisoned the attitudes of other members. He was critical of the captains and soon another member, Private Newman, joined in with Reed. Both were arrested and tried at a court martial. Newman's punishment was to be "discarded," language representing a severe and personal rebuke for his behavior.

Every day, Lewis could be seen making observations in his journal, carrying his rifle and trusty espontoon (a combination sword and rod that could be used to mount his rifle for stable shooting). One day, as Lewis walked along the steep cliffs, he slipped and was headed toward a three-hundred-foot fall into the river below. Just as he was about to go down, he thrust his knife into the hillside and pulled himself to safety.

Meanwhile, one of the key leaders, Sergeant Floyd, had grown increasingly ill. By August 20, he died from what now appears to have been an infected appendix. They buried him at a beautiful bluff along the river and named it Floyd's Bluff in his honor.

On August 27, they met the Yankton Sioux who approached the party in full regalia and four musicians. They seemed to have a sense of the dramatic, but proved to be very friendly. Lewis and Clark offered them presents but the chiefs wanted ammunition. The captains tended to negotiate with only one chief (whomever they perceived as the primary leader) which proved to be a cultural offense. But the Yankton's desire for friendship overcame the expedition's ignorance. The party was invited to their ceremonial dance, and to spend the night in the village.

One day, Private Shannon failed to come back after hunting. Colter was sent out to look; when he did not return, Drouillard was sent. They found Shannon's tracks and concluded Shannon was ahead of the party, but Shannon thought he was behind, so he was racing to catch up. Shannon was not the best of hunters, so they feared he was starving and in a panic. They finally found him after a sixteen-day chase, twelve days of which Shannon had been hunting without bullets. He had killed some small animals with pointed sticks and survived on fruit and berries.

The journey was becoming complicated.

HAVING A TEAM made the expedition possible, but teams also can be the cause of difficulty. Team members can rebel against leadership. They can fight each other. Team members take up resources. They need encouragement, food, or pay. They can get bored or lazy. Like Shannon, they can get lost and take time and energy to get them back on track. Sometimes projects feel more difficult because of the participation of other people.

It is painful when setback, heartache, and failure come from those who have been committed to the vision. In war, when soldiers die at the hands of their own comrades, it is called "friendly fire." Sometimes friendly fire takes place in the Church when people criticize, create dissension and confusion, or fall into sinful behaviors.

Leaders should not be surprised to discover that their team is comprised of fallible people who fail in many ways. The Bible is full of examples.

Disagreement

Sometimes there is legitimate disagreement between people of goodwill and commitment. These situations are perplexing. Paul had wonderful friendship with his teammates, but his teammates were not without their problems. John Mark was forcibly removed from the team after his failure to follow through on the first missionary journey. This caused such a rift between Paul and Barnabas that the team broke up and the two went their separate ways (Acts 15.39).

Criticism

Moses felt the frustration of the constant complaint of the Israelites. Time after time, the people had seen the delivering work of the Lord as they were led out of Egypt. But on the brink of their destination, the land promised to Abraham, ten of the twelve spies brought a bad report, inciting rebellion among the people. The people of Israel, despite protest from Joshua and Caleb, rebelled against God and Moses, bitterly lamenting their release from slavery.

> Then all the congregation raised a loud cry, and the people wept that night. And all the people of Israel grumbled against Moses and Aaron. The whole congregation said to them, "Would that we had died in the land of Egypt! Or would that we had died in this wilderness! Why is the Lord bringing us into this land, to fall by the sword? Our wives and our little ones will become a prey. Would it not be better for us to go back to Egypt?" And they said to

one another, "Let us choose a leader and go back to Egypt."

~ Numbers 14.1-4

The despair of the leaders was dramatic. "Then Moses and Aaron fell on their faces before all the assembly of the congregation of the people of Israel" (Num. 14.5). The rebellion at Kadesh Barnea was a devastating setback for the children of Israel. How disappointing when the people rebel and progress comes to a halt.

In the New Testament, Peter felt the sting of criticism from others in the Church when he broke Jewish tradition to visit the Gentile home of Cornelius. God's people can level disapproval, even when leaders are obedient to God's direction.

Resentment

Leaders can face resentment from those closest to them. Joseph felt the betrayal of his jealous brothers, who sold him into slavery.

When David volunteered to fight Goliath, his brothers were angry at him, saying,

> "Why have you come down? And with whom have you left those few sheep in the wilderness? I know your presumption and the evil of your heart, for you have come down to see the battle."
>
> ~ 1 Samuel 17.28

Bad Advice

Team members mean well but cause problems by giving bad advice. As David prepared to fight Goliath, Saul "clothed David with his armor. He put a helmet of bronze on his head and clothed him with a coat of mail" (1 Sam. 17.38). David refused Saul's armor because he was not accustomed to them. Saul's motive's were right, but it was the wrong approach.

Betrayal

The grief from betrayal can be the most devastating of Internal Complications. Joshua wandered the desert for forty years in bitter disappointment after the rebellion at Kadesh Barnea. Now, under his leadership, he experienced another gut-wrenching setback. On the heels of the spectacular victory at Jericho, the Israelites were routed at Ai, due to the disobedience of Achan. Although the Israelites were clearly instructed not to take any plunder from Jericho, Achan secretly kept some trinkets and buried them beneath his tent. God revealed to Joshua that Achan's sin was the cause of Israel's defeat (Josh. 7).

The classic case of Internal Complications is the one whose name is synonymous with betrayal: Judas Iscariot. One of Jesus' chosen twelve, Judas betrayed the Lord, handing Jesus over to arrest.

Disagreement. Criticism. Resentment. Betrayal. Bad Advice. These are some of the examples of Internal Complications that can block the progress of the Heroic Venture. It should be no surprise when they occur. God's leaders must seek his wisdom in each situation and he will help them through.[1]

Questions for Discussion

1. What were some of the Internal Complications that Meriwether Lewis faced with his team?
2. From the biblical accounts, what are some of the problems leaders faced with their teams?
3. If God called leaders to complete their project, why was there so much Internal Complication in carrying out the task?
4. In your own experience, what Internal Complications have you experienced in ministry?
5. What kind of Internal Complications should you expect to have in your own ministry? Which ones do you think will never happen? Why?

Notes

[1] For practical guidance in dealing with Internal Complications, see the following references:

Reference A - *What Is Wisdom?*
Reference B - *SET ON FIRE: A Framework for Decision Making, Problem Solving, and Project Leadership*
Reference E - *Discerning God's Will*
Reference I - *Developing Habits of Wisdom*

Fierce Opposition

Then Pharaoh said to him, "Get away from me;
take care never to see my face again,
for on the day you see my face you shall die." ~ *Exodus 10.28*

September - October 1804

On September 23, 1804, the Corps of Discovery met the dreaded Teton Sioux. Wading ominously up to their boat, the Teton led the expedition to their village. The captains were on their guard. In an earlier rendezvous with the Omaha tribe, the party was warned that the Tetons were plotting to rob them of their goods. Lewis and Clark indicated their intention to come as friends but that they would not hesitate to defend themselves if attacked. The two cultures cautiously exchanged gifts and speeches.

The chiefs seemed unimpressed with the gifts offered them, so Lewis and Clark invited them to the boat for some whiskey. When the chiefs asked for more, the captains declined and formed a party of soldiers to politely escort the chiefs to shore. The chiefs resisted and had to be forced onto a canoe. Two warriors grabbed the boat's bowline (the rope attached to the boat) and a third grabbed the mast. The chiefs said that they had not received enough gifts and demanded a canoe loaded with supplies before allowing the expedition to go on.

Clark drew his sword and ordered his men to arms. The cannon was swung around. Warriors strung their bows and aimed their guns. It was a dramatic moment. The expedition was outnumbered. This was the kind of moment Jefferson feared when he ordered Lewis to show restraint with the Indians. Lewis held the lighted taper over the cannon, ready for combat. Clark kept his sword out of its scabbard. Finally, one of chiefs, Black Buffalo, stepped forward to avert hostility.

Black Buffalo seized the bowline from the warriors and motioned them to go ashore. Others joined on the bank, even though their bows were still strung with arrows. Lewis and Clark indicated their intent to proceed. The chiefs huddled. Clark put his sword away and walked toward the chiefs with his hand extended to make peace, but the chiefs would not return the favor. Clark turned and ordered his soldiers to get in the canoe to return to the ship. The chiefs waded in after him saying they wanted to sleep on board the ship that night. Clark agreed.

The next day, the chiefs were returned to shore. Peace had been restored. The Corps of Discovery was invited into the village for an evening of celebration and dance.

After the festivities, when Clark returned to the boat to retire for the night, his canoe got out of control and slammed into the keel boat. Clark's shouting alarmed the Teton guards. In the confusion of darkness and language differences, the Tetons started shouting that they were under attack by a rival tribe. Soon, two hundred warriors lined up on the bank. Lewis put the expedition on guard with rifles primed. Soon everyone realized it was a false alarm and returned to bed.

The following morning, the bank was lined with well-armed warriors. Black Buffalo came on board the boat and asked the captains to stay another day. Before the captains could decline, some warriors grabbed the bowline. Black Buffalo insisted on receiving tobacco. Lewis felt it was a bribe that would acknowledge the Teton's right to collect a toll, so he refused.

The chief then demanded a flag and tobacco. Clark threw a tobacco carrot on the bank and demanded release as he lit the cannon's firing taper. Black Buffalo still demanded more tobacco so Lewis threw a handful on the bank. The chief grabbed the line from the warriors' hands. The confrontation was over, but they had not made a favorable impression. They barely managed to avoid disastrous exchange, raising concern about their return trip home.

The expedition continued on their way, encountering the grizzly bear for the first time. They also met the Arikara tribe, whom Lewis gathered were farmers oppressed by the Sioux. They had a good exchange and believed they could broker a mutual peace between the warring nations, which would enhance diplomacy and friendship with the United States. They offered the Arikaras whiskey but were turned down. They said "Why would you offer something to us that makes us act like fools?" They were finding that no two tribes were alike.

LEWIS KNEW the likelihood of facing tribes who would be in opposition to their passage along the Missouri River. In the same way, it is no surprise when people from outside the team stand in the way of God's projects. God's project leaders have faced Fierce Opposition in many ways.

Slander

Potiphar's wife tried to seduce Joseph, and when she was rejected, she lied about Joseph and had him put in prison.

Discouragement

Zerubbabel had been sent by King Cyrus to rebuild the temple in Jerusalem. The enemies of Judah and Benjamin who lived around Jerusalem were alarmed. They wanted to keep their power in the region and feared the Jews regaining political control. So they "bribed counselors against them to frustrate their purpose, all the days of Cyrus king of Persia, even until the reign of Darius king of Persia" (Ezra 4.5). This opposition continued in various forms for over fifteen years (overlapping the reign of two different kings)!

Death Threats

The Judges

During the days of the Judges, the Midianites, Philistines, and Ammonites were among the regional peoples seeking to destroy the Jews. This prompted Samson, Deborah, Barak, and Jephthah to action.

Moses

Pharaoh set himself like stone against Moses' repeated pleas to let the Israelites go free. When Moses and Aaron first approached Pharaoh, the king responded by punishing the Israelite slaves. God hardened Pharaoh's heart in progressive fashion, using each successive plague against the Egyptians. Finally, by the time the last plague had come, Pharaoh threatened Moses with death saying, "Get out of my sight! Make sure you do not appear before me again! The day you see my face you will die" (Exod. 10.28).

David

Goliath defied the army of the God of Israel in bold fashion, making vicious threats. His fearsome size caused Saul and his men to be "dismayed and greatly afraid" (1 Sam. 17.11). When David volunteered to fight against Goliath and approached him in battle, Goliath despised him.

> And the Philistine said to David, "Am I a dog, that you come to me with sticks?" And the Philistine cursed David by his gods. The Philistine said to David, "Come to me, and I will give your flesh to the birds of the air and to the beasts of the field."
>
> ~ 1 Samuel 17.43-44

Esther

Haman was the most powerful man in Persia, second only to King Xerxes. He hated Mordecai, the Jew who refused to bow down to Haman's conceit. Haman determined to kill not only Mordecai, but all the Jews because of Mordecai's offense. Haman deceived the king into issuing an edict that would destroy all the Jews who were in exile under the vast Persian empire.

Nehemiah

Nehemiah faced a different set of enemies when he attempted to rebuild the wall around Jerusalem. As soon as the news leaked out, Sanballat and Tobiah, regional officials, mocked and ridiculed him, saying, "Are you rebelling against the king?" (Neh. 2.19). As Nehemiah made progress, Sanballat became outraged. They joined with other Ammonites and Arabs in a plot to fight against the workers. They threatened, "They will not know or see till we come among them and kill them and stop the work." (Neh. 4.11).

Joseph and Mary

Joseph and Mary were newlyweds when they traveled to Bethlehem for a census ordered by the Roman government. Mary gave birth to Jesus and the family lived there temporarily until they could go back to Nazareth. At the same time, the magi had passed through King Herod's court seeking the king who was represented by the star they had followed. When Herod realized a rival king may have been born in Bethlehem, he ordered the slaughter of all boys under two years old. Jesus' life was spared when an angel instructed Joseph to take his family to live in Egypt until Herod died (Matt. 2.12-14).

Jesus

Jesus narrowly escaped being stoned by an angry mob (John 8.59) and was almost thrown off a cliff by those in his home town (Luke 4.39). Later in his life, he was continually resisted by Jewish leaders, who eventually had him arrested and called for his death.

Paul

When Paul first received Christ outside Damascus, his old friends became his fierce opponents and sought to kill him. To help him escape, his new friends took him by night and lowered him in a basket through an opening in the wall (Acts 9.25).

Paul also faced opposition at many cities during his missionary journeys. The Judiazers, who maintained that Gentiles must first become Jews before becoming Christians, were frequently enemies of Paul in various towns (e.g. Acts 20.3). In Jerusalem some Jews from Asia provoked a mob, leading to Paul's arrest. Two days later, a group of forty formed a conspiracy, binding themselves by an oath, not to eat or drink until they had killed Paul (Acts 23.12).

Although people will oppose the Heroic Venture out of selfish motives, fear, misunderstanding, or a commitment to their own cause, the real source of Fierce Opposition is the devil and the spiritual forces of evil in the heavenly realms.

We do not battle against flesh and blood (Eph. 6.12).

Questions for Discussion

1. Describe a time when you faced opposition in ministry.
2. In the biblical examples, what was the motivation to oppose God's work?
3. In the biblical examples, how did God's people react to opposition?
4. Why might people oppose the good ministry you are seeking to do?
5. If you face Fierce Opposition, how should you handle it?

Redemptive Setbacks

And the Lord had given the people favor in the sight of the Egyptians, so that they let them have what they asked. Thus they plundered the Egyptians. ~ Exodus 12.36

October 1804 - April 1805

In late October 1804, the party reached their long-expected winter quarters at the Mandan Indian village. Around five thousand Mandans came out to greet them. The dancing and socializing lasted multiple days.

To prevent problems related to idleness, the men were kept busy building a fort, repairing equipment, crafting canoes, hunting for food, and trading. They found the Mandans had great interest in the production of the crew's battle axes, barely keeping up with demand. They found the Mandans to be skilled traders who drove hard bargains.

Despite the long winter, with considerable time spent indoors, morale and discipline problems were few. The lone exception occurred when one of the men was caught climbing over the wall after curfew. This was not a grave offense except the Mandans started copying this behavior, which created a security problem. The soldier was tried and punished, although not as severely as the two who had previously been expelled from the company.

The captains continued efforts to negotiate peace between the Mandans and other Indian tribes. But peace and war had different meanings to the natives than it did for the Colonists. War among rival tribes was the best way to show leadership ability and earn political favor with current leaders. Hostilities between tribes could break out at any time which brought revenge raids. For young men, war was the primary means of political advancement. When Lewis talked about the importance of peace, one of the warriors asked, "What then would we do for the chiefs?" War was a normal way of life for many of the tribes the expedition encountered.

The Indians resented the presents offered to them, as well as the high-sounding tone that disrespected their prowess as warriors. Still, the Mandans were patient with the party. Without the Mandans food and hospitality, the Corps of Discovery would not have survived the winter. The men also gained important medical knowledge from the Indians, including a remedy for snake bites, which was later incorporated into the body of the world's medical knowledge.

The captains met a French trader named Charbonneau and hired him as an interpreter. He was married to a Shoshone woman named Sacagawea who had been kidnaped by a rival tribe and sold into slavery to the Mandans. The Shoshones were indigenous to the mountains linking the Missouri and Columbia Rivers, so it would be important to forge a friendly relationship with them.

The men were unimpressed with Charbonneau's lack of courage and character, but they held Sacagawea in high regard. Although she was ready to give birth soon, it was believed she could manage a newborn baby and join the party when they were ready to leave in the Spring.

Lewis and Clark believed Sacagawea would be helpful in negotiating the horses needed to make the portage over the western mountains. They were told that the Shoshones had plenty of horses. Having experienced the difficulty of communicating only in sign language, the captains hoped she would be a useful interpreter. In February, Sacagawea gave birth to a boy, naming him Jean Baptiste. Lewis served as the midwife and delivered the baby. The Corps of Discovery now included a Native American woman and a newborn baby.

Lewis spent considerable time getting information from Indian tribes about the next leg of the trip, which was unknown territory. Most of the intelligence about the journey was based on speculation and stories heard from various tribes. No one had actually made the trip over the mountains to the Pacific. But from what Lewis could patch together there was some clarity about what was to come next.

About 115 miles from the Mandan village was a large river. Three miles later was the Yellowstone River, then another 150 miles to the "River Which Scolds at All Others." Another 120 miles and a great noise could be heard with a fine, open plain leading to the Great Falls of Montana. After the Great Falls, there would be sixty miles to reach a mountain range. The

Missouri would split into three forks seventy-five miles into the mountains. This was the place where Sacagawea had been captured five years earlier. North of Three Forks was a navigable route to the foot of high mountains dividing the Atlantic and Pacific Oceans, which could be passed on foot in one day, it was thought, to a river on the west side.

This was exciting news. The vision of finding an easy water passage from the Atlantic to the Pacific was about to be realized. Lewis would be able to send a favorable report to Jefferson that the route to the Pacific was being found and mapped. This would be the first systematic survey of the area west of the Mississippi, a valuable contribution to the world's knowledge. Morale was high and the party was eager for winter to end so they could get back on their way.

Lewis intended to leave two canoes at the Great Falls. Then he planned to put his treasured iron boat together, the one he had spent so much time designing back in Harpers Ferry. It would have to be fortified with skins to keep it afloat, but he was hopeful it would be a success.

On April 7, 1805, part of the group was sent back to St. Louis with a report back to Washington, D.C. Later that day, the rest of the Corps of Discovery left the Mandan village heading west, ready to set out in new, uncharted terrain. They were about to penetrate a vast country of unknown width. The good or evil they might face could not be predicted. They had very few provisions. Yet they were excited because it was the moment they had been waiting for since joining the expedition. It had consumed Lewis' mind his whole adult life. Their departure was among the happiest days of their lives.

EVEN THOUGH the party had to winter with the Mandans, and they could not make any progress toward their destination, they tried to make the most of the situation. What appeared at first to be a "lull in the action," turned out to be quite helpful to their overall mission. During their winter's inactivity, they gathered vital intelligence about the journey ahead and added invaluable members to the crew, most notably Sacagawea.

In the same way, God takes what seem like setbacks, and uses them to actually strengthen the leader's ability to complete the project.

Samson

Samson's parents were unable to have children until an angel foretold Samson's miraculous conception. They were to set Samson apart as a Nazirite for the purpose of delivering Israel from the Philistines. As Samson grew, the Lord blessed him and the "Spirit of the Lord began to stir him" (Judg. 13.25).

Obedient to God's instruction, Samson's parents must have been appalled by Samson's first recorded act. Samson said, "I saw one of the daughters of the Philistines at Timnah. Now get her for me as my wife" (Judg. 14.2).

Instead of defeating the Philistines people, he was marrying into them! His parents asked, "Is there not a woman among the daughters of your relatives, or among all our people, that you must go to take a wife from the uncircumcised Philistines?" (v. 3). But Samson was convinced that this was the woman for him.

What the parents did not know is that God was planning to redeem this situation as a way to infiltrate the Philistines from within (v. 4). A disappointment to Samson's parents was an opportunity for God.

God's final act of redemption in Samson's life came when he had been imprisoned and humiliated by the Philistines. Robbed of his eyesight by the Philistines, Samson finally was listening to God. Samson was now focused on his assignment: to bring revenge against the Philistines and deliver Israel. Although he had defeated many Philistines throughout his lifetime, Samson was ready to give what remained of his life to finishing his task.

But the circumstances seemed like a permanent setback for Samson. Chained to two pillars in the Philistine temple, without sight, and without his notable strength, he was an object of scorn from the leaders sitting in the temple mocking him. Samson prayed for one last opportunity for strength. "Then he bowed with all his strength, and the house fell upon the lords and upon all the people who were in it. So the dead whom he killed at his death were more than those whom he had killed during his life" (Judg. 16.30). God redeemed what looked like a hopeless setback.

Joseph

Joseph was a favored son among the twelve sons of Israel. Joseph had a vision about his future leadership, implying that his brothers would one day bow down to him. When he brashly reported this vision to his jealous brothers, they sold him into Egyptian slavery. This was a serious setback, at least in Joseph's mind.

But God had plans to redeem the situation. God's assignment for Joseph was to save the Israelites from the upcoming famine. In order for this to happen, Joseph would need to move to Egypt and be placed in a position of influence. God also used this setback to develop Joseph's character. Joseph needed to be disciplined to blunt the edges of his arrogance. He needed to be made humble in order for God to use him. Being sold into slavery accomplished both aims: he was physically transplanted to his assignment in Egypt, and was humbled in the process.

Joseph eventually understood that God was the author of this Redemptive Setback. Many years later, when Joseph had reached the pinnacle of power as governor in Egypt, Joseph's brothers miraculously visited him. Joseph was the only one who could sell them grain to help them in this time of famine. Joseph recognized his brothers, but his brothers did not recognize him. When Joseph finally revealed himself, the brothers were afraid because of their past betrayal. Their fear grew to terror when they realized the authority Joseph now wielded in Egypt.

Joseph calmed their fears because he understood the redemptive nature of God's plan. He said to his brothers:

> I am your brother, Joseph, whom you sold into Egypt. And now do not be distressed or angry with yourselves because you sold me here, for God sent me before you to preserve life. For the famine has been in the land these two years, and there are yet five years in which there will be neither plowing nor harvest. And God sent me before you to preserve for you a remnant on earth, and to keep alive for you many survivors.
>
> ~ Genesis 45.4-7

Later, when their father Jacob died, the brothers were again moved to fear Joseph's revenge. They sent word to Joseph to forgive them for the sins and wrongs they committed in treating him so badly (Gen. 50.17). When Joseph received this message, he wept. He replied to them in kindness saying, "As for you, you meant evil against me, but God meant it for good, to bring it about that many people should be kept alive, as they are today" (Gen. 50.20).

When leaders accept the assignment God gives them, and keep their focus on that vision, even setbacks at the hands of others can be seen as redemptive. People can respond with grace and forgiveness.

Moses and The Exodus

Moses was given his project at the burning bush. God revealed that Pharaoh would not immediately release Israel, saying:

> So I will stretch out my hand and strike Egypt with all the wonders that I will do in it; after that he will let you go. And I will give this people favor in the sight of the Egyptians; and when you go, you shall not go empty, but each woman shall ask of her neighbor, and any woman who lives in her house, for silver and gold jewelry, and for clothing. You shall put them on your sons and on your daughters. So you shall plunder the Egyptians.
>
> ~ Exod. 3.20-22

God had a plan to rescue his people, but also to send them on their way with the riches of Egypt. In order to do this, however, the people would need to experience what would appear as a setback. The Israelites would have to face more hardships that would seem to take them backward, rather than forward.

God revealed, "I will harden his heart, so that he will not let the people go" (Exod. 4.21). When Pharaoh first heard Moses and Aaron plead for release, Pharaoh ordered the slaves to make the same quota of bricks, this time without a supply of straw. When Moses and Aaron returned from their meeting with Pharaoh, the Israelites were there waiting. In anger they said to Moses, "The Lord look on you and judge, because you have made us stink in the sight of Pharaoh and his servants, and have put a sword in their hand to kill us" (Exod. 5.21).

Moses said to the Lord:

> O Lord, why have you done evil to this people? Why did you ever send me? For since I came to Pharaoh to speak in your name, he has done evil to this people, and you have not delivered your people at all.
>
> ~ Exodus 5.22-23

Moses had not yet understood that God was using this setback to achieve his purposes. It would take ten plagues before the Egyptians' will would be broken to the point of giving away their treasures to the Hebrews.

Finally, when the plague of the firstborn was visited on the Egyptians, Pharaoh released the Israelites, saying, "Up, go out from among my people, both you and the people of Israel; and go, serve the Lord, as you have said. Take your flocks and your herds, as you have said, and be gone" (Exod. 12.31-32). The Egyptian people were also eager to see them leave. "For otherwise," they said, "we will all die!" (Exod. 12.33, NIV).

The Israelites did as Moses instructed and asked the Egyptians for articles of silver and gold and for clothing. "And the Lord had given the people favor in the sight of the

Egyptians, so that they let them have what they asked. Thus they plundered the Egyptians" (Exod. 12.36).

The Israelites saw the plagues as a series of setbacks, but God knew it was all part of the plan to give the people "favor in the sight of the Egyptians" (Exod 12.36). They were equipped with the treasure and supplies they would need later in their formation as a nation and culture entering the Promised Land.

Paul

Paul was traveling on his second missionary journey when his team tried to enter the province of Asia and Bithynia, but "the Spirit of Jesus did not allow them" (Acts 16.7). When Paul received a vision of a man begging him to come to Macedonia, he concluded God was calling him to preach there (Acts 16.10). Traveling with Silas, Paul went to the leading city in that district of Macedonia, called Philippi. Given the dramatic leading he felt a few days earlier, Paul was probably eager to see what God had in store for them in Macedonia.

While in Philippi, Paul and Silas encountered a slave girl who made her masters rich by telling fortunes. The girl harassed Paul and Silas by continuously following them, shouting, "These men are servants of the Most High God, who proclaim to you the way of salvation" (Acts 16.17).

After many days of this, Paul had enough and commanded the evil spirit to come out of her. She was healed, but also lost her fortune-telling ability. When the owners realized their money-making machine was gone, they seized Paul and Silas, and took them to the marketplace to face the authorities. When a mob formed, the officials had Paul and Silas beaten and thrown in prison, placing their feet in stocks, giving instructions to the jailer to keep them under heavy guard.

What happened? Paul had received a clear vision to go to Macedonia and the first place he went landed him in prison. But Paul and Silas did not show signs of despair. At midnight they were praying and singing hymns to God, as the other prisoners listened. Suddenly, an earthquake caused the doors to open and their chains fell off. In a panic, the jailer was about to kill himself for letting the prisoners escape, but Paul shouted, "Do not harm yourself, for we are all here" (Acts 16.28).

As a result of their testimony and the earthquake, the jailer and his whole household received Christ and were baptized that very night. God used what looked like a setback to bring a whole family to Christ.

Years later, when Paul was arrested in Jerusalem, he could have seen it as an end to his ministry. But God had redemptive plans in mind. God told Paul, "Take courage, for as you have testified to the facts about me in Jerusalem, so you must testify also in Rome" (Acts 23.11).

Setbacks come in various forms. Samson, Joseph, and Paul were in prison. Moses and the Israelites were enslaved in a foreign land. No matter what the circumstances, God is at work in Redemptive Setbacks, accomplishing his purposes in the Heroic Venture.

Questions for Discussion

1. Describe a time when you faced a setback and felt like giving up.
2. Lewis and Clark were forced to stop their progress up the Missouri because of winter conditions. How did they make use of this time to make a significant contribution to their vision?
3. How did God make use of serious setbacks in the lives of Joseph, Moses, and Paul?
4. How was God able to redeem Samson's reckless behavior for his glory?
5. What kind of setbacks might you experience in your ministry? How should you react if these things happen?

Painful Suffering

. . . in toil and hardship, through many a sleepless night,
in hunger and thirst, often without food,
in cold and exposure. ~ 2 Corinthians 11.27

April - May 1805

The party was only a few days out from the Mandan Village
before unforeseen obstacles began. The absence of timber
from the landscape was becoming a problem. Lewis said, "The
country is one continued level fertile plain as far as the eye can
reach in which there is not even a solitary tree or shrub." To the
eastern settler, a treeless plain would be viewed as bad for
agriculture. Only a wooded area was good for growing things.

The sight of a prairie without trees was also unsettling. They
had never seen it. The joke was that a squirrel could jump from
tree to tree from the Atlantic to the Mississippi without touch-
ing the ground.[1] Therefore, a prairie without trees was a new
and fearful sight.

It also created a practical problem. The party needed wood to
fuel their campfires. Later they would need trees to provide
pitch to hold the skins on the modular iron boat Lewis had so
carefully constructed in Harpers Ferry in 1803.

Food was sometimes scarce. Sacagawea, carrying her newborn baby (nicknamed "Pomp" by the crew), was talented in finding wild artichokes and roots that kept the men alive.

Strong head winds slowed them down and even forced the party to stay in camp a whole day. They used the time to dry out damp articles, make repairs to shoes and clothes, and add to the meat supply. The captains caught up on their journaling and made celestial observations.

Despite their challenges, the group continued to feel alert and alive. They were entering the most unknown part of their journey, but these unknowns brought out their fullest creative talents. Their journals were full of scientific information and descriptions about their surroundings. Their health was good, their ambition boundless and determination complete.

By April 25, 1805 they reached the Yellowstone River, just where the Indians told them it would be. A dram of whiskey was issued to celebrate the event and the evening was spent singing and dancing, forgetting past toils. Next, they expected a clear run on the Missouri to the base of the Rocky Mountains, followed by a one-day march over the mountains.

By May 9, the Rocky Mountains could be seen in the distance. At 5:00 p.m. Private Bratton was seen running and making frantic signs. Out of breath, he explained that he had shot and wounded a grizzly bear that pursued him a considerable distance. The men went out after it and shot it multiple times until it finally died.

Three days later another bear was encountered. Four men fired their rifles at the same time with two guns held in reserve (back then it took about two minutes to reload and prepare to fire again). The bear rose with a roar and launched a counterattack. The two reserve guns were fired, slowing the bear only for an instant. The men took flight, some to the boats, and others into hiding. The bear was shot several more times but that only helped the bear know where to chase the men. Two men abandoned their rifles and dove into river. The bear jumped in and was about to reach them when another shot was fired that finally killed it. Upon examination, it had taken eight bullets to kill the bear. The men had new respect for the grizzly bear.

Shortly after, Charbonneau was at the helm of the boat when a sudden squall hit and almost overturned it. Charbonneau panicked, and the boat filled up to within an inch of sinking. From the shore, Lewis watched in horror as precious cargo, journals, maps, instruments, and supplies started to drift away. Lewis held these items in higher regard than his own life. He wrote in his journal, "If they had been lost, I should have valued my life but little." Cruzatte threatened to shoot Charbonneau if he did not regain his composure and right the boat.

Meanwhile, Sacagawea was calm and collected. She responded with resolution and fortitude, gathering up the articles that were drifting away. Once again she proved her worth to the expedition, while disrespect toward her husband grew. With everything accounted for, they thought it a proper occasion to console themselves with a drink of grog.

The hills and cliffs they passed were exquisite. They were 200-300 feet high and nearly perpendicular, shining almost pure white in the sun. On May 26, Lewis climbed a bluff and had the first full view of the Rocky Mountains, bringing a fresh joy to his heart. His was the pleasure of finding himself so near the source of the Missouri River, but also the dismay of the difficulties that lay ahead. The snowy barrier would provide suffering and hardship for the party. Beneath the joy and dismay was a deeper sense of resolution and optimism. Lewis said, "As I have always held it a crime to anticipate evils, I will believe it a good comfortable road until I am compelled to believe differently."

With the mountains in view, the desire to get over them intensified. But progress was slower than ever because of frequent bends in the river, head-on winds, shallow water, and protruding rocks. The men had to pull the boats by hand. The water was cold on their legs, the sun hot on their backs. Their footing was either slippery and muddy or the rocks cut and bruised their feet. Walking on shore was difficult because cactus thorns easily penetrated their thick moccasins.

The nights were cold, rainy, and miserable. They often slept in watery beds. The mosquitoes were the worst plague of all, getting in their teeth, ears, and mouths. Even Lewis' Newfoundland dog, who accompanied the party, howled all night from the constant swarm of mosquitoes. Lewis also got dysentery and could not proceed for a few days until a strong laxative brought relief.

THE PARTY experienced many kinds of suffering along the way. In the military, these difficulties are called privation. Napoleon Bonaparte, the famous French general, said:

> "The most important qualification of a soldier is fortitude under fatigue and privation. Courage is only second; hardship, poverty and want are the best school for a soldier."[2]

The Heroic Venture sometimes involves Painful Suffering, such as persecution, danger, pain, hot weather, cold weather, financial problems, lack of sleep, criticism, false accusation, or imprisonment. In the Bible, God's leaders encountered suffering of many kinds.

Material Sacrifice
Abraham gave up the safety and security of his father's home in Ur and set out for a land he knew nothing about. His future well-being was uncertain.

Nehemiah sacrificed financially for the good of the cause. For twelve years as governor, neither Nehemiah nor his close relatives ate the food allotted to them, even though earlier governors taxed the people heavily to pay for their food and wine. He said:

> "But I did not do so, because of the fear of God. I also persevered in the work on this wall, and we

acquired no land, and all my servants were gathered there for the work."

~ Nehemiah 5.15-16

Persecution

In Hebrews 11.35-38, the heroes of faith faced many kinds of hardship, but they were willing to be obedient to God, even to the point of death. They were:

> tortured, refusing to accept release, so that they might rise again to a better life. Others suffered mocking and flogging, and even chains and imprisonment. They were stoned, they were sawn in two, they were killed with the sword. They went about in skins of sheep and goats, destitute, afflicted, mistreated—of whom the world was not worthy—wandering about in deserts and mountains, and in dens and caves of the earth.

The Apostles' Suffering

Paul described every kind of Painful Suffering the apostles experienced in the fulfillment of their mission. He said:

> "But as servants of God we commend ourselves in every way: by great endurance, in afflictions, hardships, calamities, beatings, imprisonments, riots, labors, sleepless nights, hunger."

~ 2 Corinthians 6.4-5

And he went on to give his credentials as an apostle:

> Are they servants of Christ? I am a better one—I am talking like a madman—with far greater labors, far more imprisonments, with countless beatings, and often near death. Five times I received at the hands of the Jews the forty lashes less one. Three times I was beaten with rods. Once I was stoned. Three times I was shipwrecked; a night and a day I was adrift at sea; on frequent journeys, in danger from rivers, danger from robbers, danger from my own people, danger from Gentiles, danger in the city, danger in the wilderness, danger at sea, danger from false brothers; in toil and hardship, through many a sleepless night, in hunger and thirst, often without food, in cold and exposure.
>
> ~ 2 Corinthians 11.23-27

The Apostle Peter warned Christians to be ready for Painful Suffering. He said:

> "Beloved, do not be surprised at the fiery trial when it comes upon you to test you, as though something strange were happening to you. But rejoice insofar as you share Christ's sufferings, that you may also rejoice and be glad when his glory is revealed."
>
> ~ 1 Peter 4.12-13

The Example of Jesus

Jesus himself was "despised and rejected by men; a man of sorrows, and acquainted with grief" (Isa. 53.3). He "did not count equality with God a thing to be grasped, but made himself nothing, taking the form of a servant" (Phil. 2.6-7). In order to complete his mission he gave up the stability of home to become a traveling preacher. He said, "Foxes have holes, and birds of the air have nests, but the Son of Man has nowhere to lay his head" (Luke 9.58).

In the final part of Christ's mission, he suffered a terrible beating followed by vicious execution on the cross. No one knew Painful Suffering like Jesus. But even in light of Jesus' difficulties, he encouraged his disciples, saying, "In the world you will have tribulation. But take heart; I have overcome the world" (John 16.33).

Painful Suffering is productive in the Heroic Venture. Paul said, "We must go through many hardships to enter the kingdom of God" (Acts 14.22, NIV) and that "we rejoice in our sufferings, knowing that suffering produces endurance, and endurance produces character, and character produces hope" (Rom. 5.3-4).

Questions for Discussion

1. Peter said we should not be "surprised at the fiery trial when it comes upon you to test you, as though something

strange were happening to you." Give some examples of times you find yourself surprised that you suffer.

2. When you look at the biblical examples of the suffering of God's servants, how do you feel? Do you feel frightened, inspired, angered, confused?
3. How does God view the suffering of his project leaders?
4. What kinds of Painful Suffering might you expect in your ministry?
5. How prepared do you feel to endure the suffering that awaits you as you pursue your vision?

Notes

[1] Burns, Ken. 1997. *Lewis and Clark: The Journey of the Corps of Discovery*. Burbank, CA: PBS Home Video.

[2] Charlton, James, ed. 2002. *The Military Quotation Book*. New York: St. Martin's Press, page 12.

Confident Command

*Joshua commanded the officers of the people, "Pass through
the midst of the camp and command the people,
'Prepare your provisions.'" . . . And they answered Joshua,
"All that you have commanded us we will do."* ~ Joshua 1.10, 16

June 1805

At dusk on June 2, 1805, the party pulled onto the south shore
of the Missouri River. Across the water they could see two considerable rivers flowing into the Missouri. The Indians, whose
information had been accurate so far, had said nothing about
this confluence of two rivers. The Great Falls were to be the
next landmark. It was too dark to explore, but this created a
crisis that required a difficult decision for the captains.

Which of the two rivers was the Missouri? The north fork or the
south fork? Lewis was astonished that such an important item
was omitted from the Indians' intelligence. Jefferson's orders
were explicit: "the object of your mission is to explore the
Missouri River." So making the right decision was critical to
the venture. They were at the proverbial fork in the road.

The north fork was deeper. It ran in the same boiling and roll-
ing manner which had uniformly characterized the Missouri so
far. Its waters were of a whitish brown color, very characteristic
of the Missouri. The south fork was perfectly transparent and

ran with a smooth surface. Its current was swifter than the north fork.

The air and character of the north fork was so precisely like that of the Missouri that the whole party (with two exceptions) firmly believed it to be the Missouri. The two exceptions were captains Lewis and Clark. Each side was equally firm in their belief.

Lewis reasoned the north fork had run an immense distance through the plains to pick up enough sediment to make it so cloudy, leading him to conclude that the south fork must have come directly out of the mountains. The bed of the south fork was composed of smooth stones like most rivers issuing from mountainous country, while the bed of the north fork was mainly mud. Despite their confidence, Lewis and Clark decided to split up and explore each river to see if more evidence could be found.

As Lewis passed across a bluff, he slipped at a narrow walkway, going straight down a craggy precipice of 90 feet, saving himself with his espontoon. He just barely managed to reach a place where he could stand with some safety.

Before catching his breath he heard Private Windsor cry out "Captain, what shall I do?" Lewis turned and saw Windsor, overwhelmed with fear, lying prostrated on his belly, holding on as best he could with his left arm and foot, his right hand arm and leg hanging over the same precipice Lewis had just passed. Lewis was afraid that Windsor could loose strength and slip off. Lewis spoke calmly, telling Windsor to take his knife from his belt and dig a hole in the face to receive his right foot. Windsor did as instructed and raised himself to knees. Lewis then instructed him to take off his slippery moccasins to crawl forward. He did so and escaped unharmed.

After their short explorations, the two groups rejoined. The men continued to believe the north fork was the real Missouri. Lewis was so sure the south fork was right, he named the north fork "Marias," in honor of his cousin. The captains tried once more to convince the men that the south fork was correct, but without success. To a man they were firm in their belief, and despite their certainty, the men cheerfully said they were ready to follow wherever Lewis and Clark thought proper.

They split up again, to look for the Great Falls. The captains wanted to make one more attempt to make sure the south fork was right, honoring the input of the group. They decided to leave one boat behind secured on an island. This would lighten the load and provide them with a supply depot on their return voyage.

On June 13, Lewis, who was moving up the south fork, reached a beautiful level plain of at least fifty to sixty miles with infinitely more buffalo than he had ever witnessed. He heard the sound of a fall of water and saw spray rise above the plain like a column of smoke. At noon he reached the Great Falls. This confirmed the captains' decision that the south fork was the Missouri.

The Indians told them there would be five miles of rapids above the Great Falls, followed by a second set of falls half as large as the first. Lewis' explorations of the Falls indicated there were *five* separate falls of the Missouri, not two. The portage around the falls was going to be more difficult than first imagined.

LEWIS AND CLARK involved the whole expedition in the critical decision about which was the right river. But when it came time to make the decision, the captains were ready to act on their best judgment, even though every member of the crew disagreed with their decision.

Effective ministry leaders work hard to listen to the team and get team members involved by participating in decision making. They know that team members respond best when given the opportunity to give input, even if the decision does not go their way. But in the end, good leaders know they must make the right decision, even if it is unpopular.

Leadership Is Representation

My colleague, Dr. Don L. Davis, has argued for a paradigm of leadership that he calls "Leadership is Representation." He defines leadership as "the ability to receive authority from another to stand in their stead."[1] In other words, every leader is under the authority of someone. Good leaders are committed to represent those who sent them. Lewis and Clark were acting on behalf of their commander-in-chief, Thomas Jefferson. Jesus was focused on pleasing the Father (John 5.19-20). Project leaders make Confident Command decisions knowing they have been trusted to serve the wishes of the leaders above them.

Submission

Confident Command instills trust and assurance in the team members. When it was time to move on, the team was behind the captains' decision. When leaders keep the vision in mind and make firm decisions in light of the vision, it helps the team followers to do the same. When everyone is focused on the vision, it becomes easier to submit to leadership:

> Obey your leaders and submit to them, for they are keeping watch over your souls, as those who will have to give an account. Let them do this with joy and not with groaning, for that would be of no advantage to you.
>
> ~ Hebrews 13.17

Sarah was a good example, as she submitted to Abraham as Abraham followed God. Sarah "obeyed Abraham and called him her master" (1 Pet. 3.6, NIV).

Defining Reality

The first job of a leader is to define reality.[2] Leaders care for their team by giving clear direction, making sure everyone knows what is happening, and clarifying what the future might hold.

In the Bible, leaders proved their ability to cut through confusing nuance, communicate with their team, and make confident decisions in the face of uncertainty.

Well-Intentioned Advice

Paul listened carefully to his friends but was not deterred from taking the action he thought best. Luke tells the story about a prophet from Judea who took Paul's belt, tied his own hands and feet with it and said, "Thus says the Holy Spirit, 'This is how the Jews at Jerusalem will bind the man who owns this belt and deliver him into the hands of the Gentiles'" (Acts 21.11). Paul's associates pleaded with him to change his plan to go to Jerusalem.

Paul answered, "What are you doing, weeping and breaking my heart? For I am ready not only to be imprisoned but even to die in Jerusalem for the name of the Lord Jesus" (v. 13). When it was clear that Paul would not change his mind, they gave up and said, "Let the will of the Lord be done" (v. 14). Despite their good intentions and the clear message from the Holy Spirit about the results of his decision, Paul had solid conviction about what he should do.

Jesus was another leader who received well-intentioned advice. After word came to him about the illness of his friend Lazarus, Jesus told his disciples, "Let us go back to Judea." They replied, "But Rabbi, a short while ago the Jews tried to stone you, and yet you are going back there?" Jesus was intent on going, and after more discussion, he concluded they would go on to Judea. Thomas showed his loyalty to Jesus' leadership, saying to the other disciples, "Let us also go, that we may die with him." Jesus listened to their concerns, but made a confident decision, while his men showed their loyalty to his Confident Command.

Loyalty

Leaders should receive loyalty from their team. Followers should expect clarity and direction from their leaders. Joshua, Gideon, Nehemiah, and Jephthah were good examples of leaders giving clear direction, and their followers' response showed their respect for leadership:

> Joshua commanded the officers of the people, "Pass through the midst of the camp and command the people, 'Prepare your provisions.'" . . . And they answered Joshua, "All that you have commanded us we will do."
> ~ Joshua 1.10, 16

Gideon received God's direction, and the people responded when the Midianites and other eastern peoples joined forces and crossed the Jordan into Israel.

> But the Spirit of the Lord clothed Gideon, and he sounded the trumpet, and the Abiezrites were called out to follow him. And he sent messengers throughout all Manasseh, and they too were called out to follow him. And he sent messengers to Asher,

113

Zebulun, and Naphtali, and they went up to meet them.

~ Judges 6.34-35

Nehemiah explained his intent to do the work, and the people responded by saying, "Let us rise up and build" (Neh. 2.18). They were ready to begin right away under his leadership.

Jephthah, when asked to lead Israel, verified the people's willingness to serve under his leadership before he accepted command. He had been sent into exile years before and now he doubted their willingness to follow. He said, "If you bring me home again to fight with the Ammonites, and the Lord gives them over to me, I will be your head." His recruiters responded by saying, "The Lord will be witness between us, if we do not do as you say" (Judg. 11.9-10). For Confident Command to be effective, there must be loyalty from the followers.

Encouragement

Sometimes, when delegating authority, people need extra encouragement. Deborah was leader over Israel when she summoned Barak and said:

Go, gather your men at Mount Tabor, taking 10,000 from the people of Naphtali and the people of Zebulun. And I will draw out Sisera, the general of Jabin's army, to meet you by the river Kishon

with his chariots and his troops, and I will give him
into your hand.

~ Judges 4.6-7

But Barak balked; he would only go on the recruiting
mission if Deborah promised to go with him. So Deborah
went with him and the ten thousand men followed Barak
into battle where Sisera was completely defeated.

Conflict Resolution

Nehemiah was an effective leader who could resolve
conflict with confidence. The people complained that they
were going hungry because their Jewish brothers were
charging outrageous interest rates for their land mortgages.
Families were not able to keep up with the payments and
were starving. Some had even sold their daughters into
slavery to make ends meet. The poor were powerless to act
since the fields and vineyards belonged to the mortgage
holders.

When Nehemiah heard these charges, he was outraged and
took action. He told the lenders:

> You are exacting interest, each from his brother. . . .
> The thing that you are doing is not good. Ought you
> not to walk in the fear of our God to prevent the
> taunts of the nations our enemies? Moreover, I and
> my brothers and my servants are lending them
> money and grain. Let us abandon this exacting of
> interest. Return to them this very day their fields,

their vineyards, their olive orchards, and their houses, and the percentage of money, grain, wine, and oil that you have been exacting from them.

~ Nehemiah 5.7, 9-11

The lenders responded, saying, "We will restore these and require nothing from them. We will do as you say" (v.12).

Still not completely satisfied, Nehemiah brought in the priests to join the group and made them take an oath, threatening God's punishment on those who did not keep their promise. "And all the assembly said 'Amen' and praised the Lord. And the people did as they had promised" (Neh. 5.13). Nehemiah was able to bring peaceful resolution to the conflict through his Confident Command.

Clarity of Command

Jesus moved confidently through the process of completing his mission. On many occasions he made it clear what was coming: "the Son of Man must suffer many things and be rejected by the elders and the chief priests and the scribes and be killed, and after three days rise again" (Mark 8.31). One time, Peter took Jesus aside and began to rebuke him. But Jesus turned to the other disciples and rebuked Peter, saying, "Get behind me, Satan! For you are not setting your mind on the things of God, but on the things of man" (Mark 8.33). Jesus was confident in his command.

In the end, every project leader must make clear decisions that are consistent with the vision. In the Heroic Venture, there must be Confident Command.

Questions for Discussion

1. If teamwork is so important (see chapter 5), why is leadership important?
2. Using the examples of project leaders in the Bible, what are three key characteristics of Christlike, biblical leadership? What do good leaders do?
3. How did God's project leaders both listen to counsel and make confident decisions?
4. How did God's project leaders use their vision and calling as the central source of their decision making?
5. What will be the keys to help you make wise decisions in your ministry?

Notes

[1] Davis, Don. 2003. *World Impact Focus and Identity*. Lake Hughes, CA: World Impact Press.

[2] DePree, Max. 1989. *Leadership Is An Art*. New York, NY: Dell Publishing, page 11.

Creative Adjustments

The people are still too many. Take them down to the water,
and I will test them for you there. ~ Judges 7.4

June 1805

On June 14, 1805, Lewis was walking along the shore making observations, feasting on the beauty of the landscape. He killed a buffalo for dinner, and as he stood there relishing the view, he forgot to reload his rifle. Suddenly, a grizzly bear came upon him leaving him no time to reload his gun. The bear was twenty steps away and advancing. There was no tree in sight and the river was only three feet deep. When the bear opened its mouth, Lewis started to run toward the river, losing ground as he went. Reaching the river, Lewis drew his espontoon and raised it. Suddenly the bear wheeled around and retreated. Lewis determined to never again leave his gun unloaded.

Lewis was barely out of the river when he saw three buffalo bulls running full speed at him. Not sure what to do, Lewis decided to charge at them head-on. When they were within one hundred yards of Lewis, the bulls stopped and turned away. It was an eventful day.

On June 16, Sacagawea became ill with a fever, irregular breathing, and alarming twitching of the fingers and arms. The key to a friendly negotiation with the Shoshone Indians, she was the expedition's best hope for a successful passage over the mountains to the Columbia River. Sacagawea was also a respected and beloved member of the team, having proved her worth on many occasions. She, and baby Pomp, had become dear to all the men.

Lewis' medical treatment was remarkable, probably beyond what any physician of his day could do, and yet without proper supplies. Within a couple of days she was better, but then she ate some raw fish and apples against her doctor's orders and her fever returned. Lewis rebuked Charbonneau severely for not watching over Lewis' patient. Lewis treated her again and in two days she was better.

Still looming ahead were the unknown mountains, which, as they drew closer, grew greater, higher, and deeper than anything ever seen in the east. They realized that Jefferson's assumptions about their height was grossly in error, but they were eager to vault over the mountains before winter set in.

First they had to deal with the reality of at least a sixteen-mile portage around the Great Falls over rough terrain. The Indians had promised a smooth landscape, but a scouting party indicated the portage would be difficult because of deep ravines. They decided to store another boatload of items for the return trip. The party split up so Clark could oversee the portage while Lewis investigated a termination point and prepared the custom-made iron boat.

On June 22, Clark's portage around the Great Falls began. There were many breakdowns and the cactus was troublesome. The men had to pull with all their might, with wheels catching on grass and stones. They were assaulted by hail the size of apples, ferocious mosquitoes, hot sun, and cold rain. The winds were fierce. Bears came close to camp at night. They grew faint and their feet were sore, but they continued cheerfully on.

Although they were entering the most dangerous part of the voyage, there was no complaining, only resolution and determination. The party knew they were making history and that this would be the most exciting and important time of their lives. They were linked by an uncommon experience and a keen sense of dependence upon one another. By now they knew each others' strengths and weaknesses; who could start the best fires, who could shoot the best, who liked which foods, where each person came from, and what their hopes and dreams were for the future. The party was fully committed to the vision. They would succeed, or die in the attempt.

Months earlier, when he accepted co-command with Lewis, Clark seemed prophetic when he said, "I will cheerfully join you and partake of the dangers, difficulties, and fatigues and I anticipate the honors and rewards of the result of such an enterprise." Together they were living out the triumph and heartbreak of such a monumental task carried out in tight-knit community. Like many soldiers who experience hardship together, they were developing close bonds of friendship.

By June 30, however, Lewis was getting impatient. They were not keeping pace to reach the Rockies. They had to give up their original idea of reaching the Pacific and returning to winter with the Mandans. They even concluded they would not be able to winter with the Shoshones.

The captains' original plan was to send three men back to St. Louis to report from the Great Falls. But the expedition was getting too far behind schedule and they could not count on a friendly reception by the Shoshones. They needed the full complement of people going forward, and a party of only three might be too small to survive an attack from the Sioux. It seemed wise to keep the party intact. Their conditions required significant adjustments to their plans.

LEWIS AND CLARK responded with Creative Adjustments to the surprises that came their way. Whether it was a grizzly bear, a buffalo, a life-threatening disease, an unexpectedly difficult portage, or getting behind schedule, the leaders of the Corps of Discovery found a way to adjust to the situation and move toward the goal.

In the same way, ministry projects are subject to every kind of surprise. No one is exempt from unforeseen circumstances. As a result, it can be said that the most important quality of project leadership is the ability to adjust to changing conditions. The Bible provides many examples.

Opposition

Jesus gave the seventy-two disciples specific instructions on how to adapt to opposition along their journey. He explained what to do when a town welcomed them, but he also knew there would be instances where they would be rejected. He said, "Whenever you enter a town and they do not receive you, go into its streets and say, 'Even the dust of your town that clings to our feet we wipe off against you'" (Luke 10.10-11). His strategy was to move on to the next town rather than persevering in the same town against clear resistance.

Nehemiah had to alter his approach when Sanballat, Tobiah, and their allies plotted against Nehemiah and his workers. Up to that point, Nehemiah had all his workers focused on building. With a changing situation he split the assignments and appointed some laborers to guard duty. He said, "We prayed to our God and set a guard as a protection against them day and night" (Neh. 4.7-9).

As the opposition was mounting, the people warned Nehemiah, "The strength of the laborers is giving out, and there is so much rubble that we cannot rebuild the wall. Wherever you turn, they will attack us." So Nehemiah adjusted again by stationing people at strategic low areas of the wall. Half the people were assigned to building, while the other half were equipped with weapons. Even those assigned to carrying materials "did their work with one hand and held a weapon in the other" (Neh. 4.10-17). Nehemiah was a master of Creative Adjustment.

God Does the Math

God seriously adjusted Gideon's strategy. After finally being convinced that God was with him, Gideon assembled an army of thirty-two thousand to defeat the Midianites. But God said to Gideon, "The people with you are too many for me to give the Midianites into their hand" (Judg. 7.4). God knew that Israel would boast about its own strength rather than give glory to God, so he instructed Gideon to send home anyone who was afraid to go to battle, leaving a force of ten thousand.

But God said the number was still too large, and he instructed Gideon to separate the men into two groups: those who lapped up water like dogs versus those who got on their knees to drink water. This reduced the army to three hundred men that God said would "save you and give the Midianites into your hand" (Judg. 7.7). Sometimes, leaders have to step out in faith with fewer resources than they think they need. God provides the victory without regard to the size of the team.

Imaginative Approaches

Samson had imaginative responses to the enemy Philistines. When his father-in-law took Samson's wife, giving her to one of the groomsmen, Samson tied a torch to the tails of three hundred foxes, bound in pairs, and sent them to destroy the Philistines' grain, olives, and vineyards (Judg. 15.4-5).

Delilah and her Philistine co-conspirators tried repeatedly to coax the secret of Samson's strength from him. Before eventually giving in to Delilah, Samson gave a series of shrewd responses that tricked the Philistines, leading to their deaths. First, he told Delilah he would lose his strength if he was tied with seven fresh bowstrings that had not been dried. Then, he claimed he could be restrained by new ropes that had never been used. Next, he told Delilah the secret was to weave the braids of his hair into the fabric of a loom and tighten them with a pin. Each time, the Philistines walked into his trap (Judg. 16.7-14).

Listening to the Father

Jesus was always ready for abrupt changes in plans, carefully following the guidance of the Father. He said:

> "The Son can do nothing of his own accord, but only what he sees the Father doing. For whatever the Father does, that the Son does likewise. For the Father loves the Son and shows him all that he himself is doing."
>
> ~ John 5.19-20

Jesus was in Galilee, staying away from Judea because he knew the Jews were waiting to take his life. When the Feast of Tabernacles arrived, Jesus' brothers urged him to go to Judea to make himself more famous, but Jesus told them the right time had not yet come. He urged them to go on to the feast without him, which they did.

Sometime after his brothers had gone, Jesus secretly went to the feast as well. He waited until half the festival was completed, then he went to the temple courts to teach publicly (John 7.1-14).

The passage does not say when Jesus decided to go to Judea, but it is reasonable to assume that the Father led Jesus to change his mind about going to the feast right after his brothers left. Jesus was ready to change plans on short notice.

Changing Strategy

Jesus was always ready to respond to the many trick questions he received from religious leaders. His enemies were on a continual hunt to get him into trouble, but he always gave an answer suited for the situation. One time, the chief priests and elders asked him:

> "By what authority are you doing these things, and who gave you this authority?" Jesus answered them, "I also will ask you one question, and if you tell me the answer, then I also will tell you by what authority I do these things. The baptism of John, from where did it come? From heaven or from man?"
>
> ~ Matthew 21.23-25

By asking this question, Jesus put his enemies on the defensive. If they said, "from heaven," then Jesus would embarrass them by asking, "then why did you not follow his teaching?" If they said, "from men," they would fear being discredited by the crowds, who held John in high regard. So the religious leaders took the cowardly way out and said, "We do not know" (Matt. 21.27). Even though Jesus was able to give a straight answer, as he had done on other occasions, asking this question revealed the true nature of their motives. Jesus provided a good example of employing a new strategy.

The devil and his demons are constantly trying to thwart God's work. As a result, leaders must be ready to set aside their plans and chart a new course when confronted with a new set of conditions. Engagement in spiritual warfare against the enemy requires listening to the Holy Spirit. It is vital to "keep in step with the Spirit" (Gal. 5.25) as leaders make Creative Adjustments in the Heroic Venture.

Questions for Discussion
1. What were some of the surprises that Lewis and Clark faced in their expedition?
2. Describe your reaction to this statement: "the most important quality of project leadership is the ability to adjust to changing conditions."
3. When the biblical project leaders needed to creatively adjust to their circumstances, how did they react?
4. In what ways was Jesus especially good at adapting his approaches?

5. What are some specific ways you can improve in your Creative Adjustment?

Dead Vision

Take your son, your only son Isaac, whom you love,
and go to the land of Moriah,
and offer him there as a burnt offering. ~ Genesis 22.2

July - August 1805

As Lewis waited for Clark to complete the miserable portage
around the Great Falls, he began the construction of his pet
project, the iron boat. The expedition was counting on the boat
to carry the bulky items down the Columbia, so a lot was at
stake. But construction was proving to be difficult. The prairie
continued to be without trees, so they had no pitch to hold the
skins together. They were forced to experiment with other
materials.

After many days of effort with beeswax and buffalo tallow the
boat was complete and placed in the river. A wind came up and
overwhelmed the boat. The skins tore and destroyed the boat.
Lewis had to relinquish his dream (many would have called it an
obsession) of the modular boat. Without the boat, substitutes
had to be found since they had stored other craft down river.

By July 12, 1805, everything was ready for departure. If the
information was right, they would meet the Shoshones and
carry their goods one day over the mountains, then float down
the Columbia River on the other side. Whatever lay ahead, they

believed it could not possibly be worse than what they had already experienced. Nothing was more arduous than the portage around the Great Falls. Nothing was more disappointing than abandoning the iron boat. The worst had to be behind them.

They were anxious to meet the Shoshones and could not figure out why they had not yet encountered them. By July 18 they decided to send Clark to look for the Shoshones. The Corps of Discovery was getting desperate.

The next day Lewis saw a column of smoke which seemed like a signal of retreat from one Shoshone party to another. They concluded the Shoshones were aware of their presence but were not willing to meet with the expedition. Their discouragement deepened.

On July 22, the men were laboring pulling canoes. Their feet often slipped and were cut on the rocks. The river bed was growing noticeably narrower and the mountains growing higher when they got a badly needed boost in morale. All of a sudden, Sacagawea recognized the section of the river. She had been there as a girl. It was the river on which Shoshones lived during the summer. The next reported landmark, "Three Forks" was close, which greatly cheered the men.

The going was tough, each day's progress measured in yards instead of miles. The mosquitoes were relentless. The river had turned southeast, so they were now going in the wrong direction. The men were weakening under the continual state of exertion. Clark returned from looking for the Shoshone, his feet bleeding and raw from prickly pears. After a day of rest, he was off again in pursuit of the elusive Shoshone.

On July 27, the party was at a breaking point when, at 9 a.m. they reached the breathtaking view of Three Forks. At 3 p.m. Clark came back into camp sick and exhausted with a fever and pain in his muscles.

The captains were anxious about the lack of contact with the Shoshones. If they did not find them and negotiate trade for horses, their voyage would be in peril. Soon they would be in the mountains with a scarce food supply, and without adequate information about the geography. They could wander in the mountains and die. Without Shoshone horses, turning back would be the best option. Still, the captains were optimistic, believing if the Indians could survive the mountains, their men could do the same.

Sacagawea informed the expedition they had reached the spot where the raiding Hidatsa tribe had taken her prisoner five years before. On August 7, they reached a junction of another set of rivers, forcing yet another decision. They were fatigued and morale was sinking fast. They hid another canoe to lighten the load. The men wanted to carry what they could on their backs and leave the rest behind but the captains thought it was unwise. They needed horses, and soon.

There was growing doubt about the navigability of the Columbia on the other side. Logic indicated the Columbia had a shorter time to descend the mountains, resulting in more waterfalls and more portages. But the captains remained hopeful. Their approach was to stay positive until events proved otherwise. They believed that when they got up to the mountain top, they would see something similar on the other side.

Lewis decided they would split up again, sending a party to find the Columbia and horses, even if it took a month. It was a do-or-die moment. Lewis continued to have unshakable confidence in his ability to find the Shoshones, and then successfully negotiate with them.

On August 9, Lewis looked through his telescope and spotted an Indian on horseback, presumably a Shoshone, about two miles ahead and coming toward him. Lewis assumed he was a scout looking for an invading Blackfoot war party. Lewis was overjoyed and knew if he could get close enough to the Indian, Lewis could prove his peaceful intent. But when they were about a mile apart, the Indian stopped. Lewis laid out a blanket on the ground as a signal of friendship.

Shields and Drouillard were accompanying Lewis along parallel paths, but out of Lewis' shouting range. Lewis was afraid to alert his party for fear of raising the Indian's suspicions. The Indian sat on his horse until Lewis was within two hundred yards. Lewis called in loud voice. Instead of responding to Lewis the Indian watched Drouillard and Shields. At one hundred yards the Indian suddenly turned his horse about, gave it the whip, leaped the creek, and disappeared in the willows, destroying all hopes of obtaining horses. Lewis was devastated.

On August 12, Lewis found a fountain representing the headwaters of the Missouri. He proceeded to the top of a dividing ridge, looked up, to the west, and saw an immense range of high mountains partially covered with snow. Lewis had the shock of finding out that there was not the one-day portage over low-lying mountains, as reported by the Indians. Instead, he was facing the towering Rocky Mountains, which were far bigger and more imposing than anything they had seen or could imagine.

Suddenly the geography of hope gave way to the geography of reality. There was no easy water route with simple portage over a gentle divide. The vision of finding an all-water route from the Mississippi to the Pacific was now dead. With this sight, decades-old assumptions about the American mountains were shattered.

The expedition was deep in Indian country, without much to trade. They had no Shoshone contacts for horses. A scout may have alerted the Shoshones to stay away from the new strangers. There was no all-water route to the Pacific, as Jefferson had hoped.

The vision was dead.

MERIWETHER LEWIS experienced the death of his vision. With the sight of the Rocky Mountains on August 12,

1805, Lewis saw his hopes to find a North American all-water route go down the drain.

Bill Gothard writes about biblical characters who experienced circumstances that put an end to their dreams. God seemed to give them a vision that raised their hopes, only to have them dashed, resulting in the death of their vision.[1]

Abraham

Abraham was told he would be the father of a great nation, that in him "all the families of the earth shall be blessed." (Gen. 12.3). After years of waiting for a son to be born in his old age, Sarah finally conceived and Isaac was born.

His vision seemed fulfilled until one day, God said to Abraham, "Take your son whom you love and sacrifice him as a burnt offering" (Gen. 22.2). Abraham took Isaac on a three-day journey to the region of Moriah, struggling with the idea of taking the life of his beloved son. Leaving his servants behind, Abraham and Isaac climbed the mountain. Abraham bound Isaac's hands and feet, laid him on the altar, and raised his knife to slay his son. (Gen. 22.1-10). Abraham faced not only the death of his vision, but also the death of his own son.

Joseph

Joseph was given a vision that his family would bow down to him. He survived being sold into slavery and prospered as Potiphar's administrator. His life was looking up. Then he was falsely accused of attacking Potiphar's wife and was thrown in prison.

While in prison, God blessed Joseph again. He found favor with the warden, who put Joseph in charge of the other prisoners. Joseph was so effective that the warden did not need to oversee Joseph's work. Among those under Joseph's administration were two prisoners sent by the king of Egypt: a cupbearer and a baker. One night, each had a different, but troubling, dream. Joseph noticed their distress and asked them why they were dejected. The men lamented that there was no one to help interpret the dreams. Joseph said, "Do not interpretations belong to God? Please tell them to me" (Gen. 40.8).

Joseph listened, then told the cupbearer the good news that the king was going to restore him to his position in three days. The baker, however, got the tragic news that he was going to be executed. Joseph pleaded with the cupbearer to seek his release when the cupbearer had audience with the king.

Just as Joseph predicted, in three days, the cupbearer was reinstated during a feast of the Pharaoh's birthday, while the baker was hanged. Joseph's hopes must have been raised. Surely, the cupbearer would advocate for him. But the cupbearer did not remember Joseph (Gen. 40.23). Forgotten, and still in prison, Joseph must have believed his vision was dead.

Moses

Moses was born four hundred years later, when the Israelites were slaves in Egypt. Miraculously rescued from Pharaoh's death order, Moses was raised by Pharaoh's daughter, receiving the world's finest education. As a member of Pharaoh's court, he had the promise of a great future.

Although Moses was raised in Pharaoh's palace, he understood that he was an Israelite. Having a sense of his destiny as rescuer of Israel, he was grieved to see his people working under forced labor. One day he saw an Egyptian beating a Hebrew. Looking around, seeing no one, he killed the Egyptian and hid the body. The next day, he saw two Israelites fighting and he intervened, serving as Hebrew protector. This time one of them said, "Who made you a prince and a judge over us? Do you mean to kill me as you killed the Egyptian?" (Exod. 2.14).

Moses was gripped with fear. His murder was public knowledge, and when Pharaoh found out, Moses became a wanted man. So Moses fled Egypt to live in Midian, 150 miles away. Moses was exposed and pursued as a fugitive. To make matters worse, his own people did not seem to appreciate his efforts to help. Now he was a stranger in a distant land, hundreds of miles from his own people, and without hope of seeing his vision completed. For forty years, Moses served as a lonely shepherd. He must have believed that his vision had died.

Jonah

Jonah was given the job of preaching to the people of Nineveh, the capital city of Assyria, an arch-enemy of Israel. The Ninevites were especially noted for their barbarous cruelty and many Israelites would have welcomed God's wrath against that wicked city. Jonah refused to preach there, knowing that God might be merciful toward them. Instead, he took a ship headed in the opposite direction. Jonah's disobedience caused a violent storm which endangered the crew, so Jonah asked to be thrown overboard to save them. As his head sunk down beneath the waves, Jonah must have believed that all of his hopes and dreams were drowning as well (Jon. 1.1-15).

Joshua

Joshua, as second in command to Moses, had seen all the miracles of the Exodus. He accompanied Moses to the mountain when God gave the Ten Commandments.

Assigned to represent his tribe as one of the twelve spies sent out to scout the Promised Land, Joshua must have been excited. He would be among the first to see the land God promised to his people after hundreds of years of Egyptian bondage.

When Joshua and Caleb returned with the other spies, their hopes were dashed by the bad report of the ten other spies. Joshua tore his clothes in anguish as he pleaded with the people to have faith and take the land. Instead of responding in faith, the people talked about stoning Moses, Joshua, Caleb, and the other leaders (Num. 14.7-10). As a result, God caused the people of Israel to wander for forty years in the desert because of their disobedience. Joshua's vision for reaching the Promised Land was dead.

The Apostles

The apostles believed that Jesus was the promised Messiah. The prophets had predicted his coming to save Israel. Even John the Baptist believed that Jesus had come to fulfill the apocalyptic prophecies about the conquering King.

When Jesus was crucified and buried, the apostles' vision died, along with Jesus. Their hopes of seeing Jesus deliver Israel were dashed.

The Heroic Venture can result in Dead Vision. How a leader responds to Dead Vision is a true test of a his or her passion and wisdom.

Questions for Discussion

1. How do you think Meriwether Lewis felt when it became apparent that his dream would not come true?
2. Which of the biblical characters can you most relate to in this chapter? Why?
3. Why does God sometimes take his people through times of Dead Vision?
4. Describe a time when you experienced the "death of a vision."

5. What should be your response if you face the death of your vision?

Notes

[1] Bill Gothard. 1979. *Basic Seminar Textbook*. Oak Brook, IL: Institute for Basic Youth Conflicts, page 150-151.

Section III: Courage to the End

"Of courage undaunted, possessing a firmness
and perseverance of purpose which nothing but
impossibilities could divert from its direction, I
could have no hesitation in confiding the
enterprise to him."

~ Thomas Jefferson's recommendation of Lewis
to command the expedition

R e n e w e d   V i s i o n

"He has risen from the dead, and behold, he is going before you to Galilee." So they departed quickly from the tomb with fear and great joy, and ran to tell his disciples. ~ Matthew 28.7, 8

August - September 1805

On August 13, 1805, the day after seeing the demoralizing view of the Rockies, Lewis' search party traveled nine more miles and stumbled upon two Indian women, an old man, and some dogs. Lewis exchanged gifts and persuaded them to take them to their tribe. Two miles later they found the sight they had long anticipated; sixty Shoshone warriors on horseback armed for war. The Shoshones halted Lewis' party, who laid down their rifles as a sign of peace. The Shoshones expected to find enemy Blackfeet warriors and would have attacked Lewis' party if not for the presence of the Indian women accompanying them. The chief approached Lewis and warmly placed his arm around him. They had finally met the Shoshones and received a friendly welcome.

While waiting for Clark's group to arrive, Lewis inquired about the passage to the Pacific. The Shoshones confirmed the way was confined by inaccessible mountains and impassable rapids so rocky that it was hopeless to pass by land or water. It was official. There was no trans-continental route, or anything remotely resembling it.

Not only was it impossible to pass by land or water, it was also out of the question to go by horse along the river. In fact, no Shoshones had ever crossed the mountains to the other side.

However, Lewis was encouraged to hear about the Nez Perce tribe, who inhabited a river on the other side of the Rockies, which was reported to "flow into a great lake of ill-tasting water toward the setting sun." This reference to the Pacific Ocean linked the continent and gave them renewed hope.

For the first time there was a known link between the oceans. The Shoshones said the Nez Perce crossed the Rockies every year to hunt buffalo on the plains, so the Nez Perce would know the best route. If the Corps of Discovery could work with the Nez Perce to find the easiest passage across the continent, part of their mission could be salvaged. There was still hope to fulfill their purpose.

Lewis was eager to hear more about what was ahead. The road was bad and there was no food so travelers had to go hungry or eat berries to stay alive. But Lewis stayed optimistic: "If others could do it, we can too." Every time they faced a bad experience, Lewis always believed that it could not possibly get worse. But it *was* looking worse. In spite of the facts, the party's motivation was still alive, and Lewis believed the men would rise to the occasion for the sake of the mission.

To move forward, Lewis needed to secure Shoshone horses and guides to get to the Nez Perce. Since the Shoshones needed guns to hunt buffalo, Lewis offered them future guns and support from the government. Negotiations almost broke down when some of the Shoshones suggested that Lewis was in alliance with their enemies and preparing an ambush. Lewis confronted them strongly, questioning their courage and challenging their manhood. The strategy worked; the horses and guides were secured, and negotiations completed.

However, Lewis was nervous that Shoshone suspicion might re-occur when the Clark party came into camp, fully armed. Wanting to lessen their fears, Lewis gave his rifle to the Chief and informed them of a Shoshone woman (Sacagawea) in Clark's party. This further inspired their confidence, so Lewis asked one of the warriors to accompany Drouillard to find Clark and bring him to camp.

When Clark arrived, a commotion broke out. Jumping Fish, one of the young Shoshone women, recognized Sacagawea. Jumping Fish was with Sacagawea the day she was abducted by the Hidatsas. The two women cried and talked all at once for a number of minutes. Then Sacagawea noticed Chief Cameahwait. She jumped into his arms and cried profusely, recognizing him as her brother! No novelist would dare invent such a scene.

IT WAS less than twenty-four hours after the death of Lewis' vision (seeing the full sight of the Rockies) that his vision was renewed. Meeting up with the Shoshones, who proved to be friendly, and having Sacagawea reconnect with her friends and family, was an amazing turn of events. The chief was even Sacagawea's brother!

Bill Gothard talks about the "supernatural fulfillment of the original vision."[1] He says, "God usually fulfills our expectations in ways we never would have thought."

Just when Lewis' vision seemed dead, new hope emerged. He gained new realization that there was a way to fulfill the vision Jefferson had entrusted to him. Renewed Vision often comes right after dreams are dashed. In the Heroic Venture, expect God to bring fresh hope in the midst of despair. It is important to keep going even when the outlook seems bleak. Renewal of vision might be just around the corner.

From Death to Life

When Abraham's knife was raised to slay his son, Isaac, an angel of the Lord called out to him from heaven, saying:

> "Abraham, Abraham! Do not lay your hand on the boy or do anything to him, for now I know that you fear God, seeing you have not withheld your son, your only son, from me."
>
> ~ Genesis 22.11-12

Abraham's faith in God was tested. God provided a ram in the thicket to serve as the sacrifice. Abraham went up Mount Moriah with a son that was as good as dead, but came back down the mountain with his vision renewed.

From Prisoner to Prime Minister

Joseph was languishing in prison with little hope of reprieve. Joseph had asked the cupbearer to remember him on the day of the cupbearer's deliverance, but the cupbearer forgot about Joseph. Two years went by, and Joseph was still in prison.

One night, Pharaoh had two dreams that troubled him. He sent for his magicians and counselors to interpret the dreams, but no one was able to do it. The controversy about Pharaoh's dreams sparked the cupbearer's memory and he remembered Joseph's ability to interpret dreams. So Pharaoh sent for Joseph to interpret the dream. Joseph replied, "It is not in me; God will give Pharaoh a favorable answer" (Gen. 41.16).

Joseph told Pharaoh that seven years of abundance was coming followed by seven years of famine, and that God was bringing this calamity soon. Joseph continued, "Now therefore let Pharaoh select a discerning and wise man, and set him over the land of Egypt" (Gen. 41.33). He went on to give other advice to help Egypt through the coming crisis. The plan seemed good to Pharaoh and his officials, so Joseph was given authority over everyone except the king. In a matter of moments, Joseph went from prisoner to prime minister. God brought Renewed Vision to Joseph's life.

From Shepherd to Deliverer

Moses was working as a shepherd in the Midian desert, 150 miles from his people in Egypt. He had once enjoyed the "treasures of Egypt" (Heb. 11.26), but now he was living an insignificant life, without hope of delivering his fellow Hebrews from Egyptian slavery.

One day, Moses was tending the flock of his father-in-law, Jethro, on the far side of the desert. Suddenly, an angel of the Lord appeared in flames of fire from a bush. When Moses approached the burning bush, God called to him, explaining Moses' assignment to deliver God's people from Egyptian slavery (Exod. 3.1-10). In one short encounter in the desert, Moses went from obscurity to being the leader of one of the greatest projects in history. Moses' vision had new life.

A Slight Reprieve

Joshua's excitement to take the Promised Land was extinguished by the Israelite rebellion at Kadesh Barnea. While the people were ready to stone Joshua, God was ready to strike the people with a plague, making Moses into a great nation. But when Moses interceded, God forgave the people and spared their lives. However, God decided against letting the rebellious people into the Promised Land. Only Caleb and Joshua would be allowed to enter.

Joshua's hope of seeing the Promised Land was restored, although there would first be forty years of wandering in the desert (one year for each of the forty days they had spied the land). The ten spies who gave the bad report were struck with a plague and died. Only Joshua and Caleb survived (Num. 14.10-38). Joshua had to persevere for decades before receiving Renewed Vision.

A Second Chance

Jonah was thrown overboard and was descending down to the depths of a watery grave. His life and ministry seemed to be at an end. But God provided a great fish to swallow Jonah for three days and nights. Jonah prayed a prayer of thanksgiving. "I called out to the Lord, out of my distress, and he answered me; out of the belly of Sheol I cried, and you heard my voice" (Jon. 2.1-2).

Jonah was given a second chance to obey God's command. The Lord commanded the fish to vomit Jonah on dry land and his mission was offered to him again. "Arise, go to Nineveh, that great city, and call out against it the message that I tell you" (Jon. 3.1). This time Jonah obeyed and preached about the destruction that was coming to Nineveh. The Ninevites believed God and repented. God saw their repentance and had compassion on them. Jonah's resurrected vision resulted in the salvation of Nineveh.

From Death to Resurrection

The apostles were devastated by Jesus' death on the cross. In fear for their lives, they hid in Jerusalem for three days, stunned by the series of events that left their world shattered. Early Sunday morning, a group of women left for the unhappy task of anointing Jesus' body at the tomb. As they approached, an angel of the Lord appeared to them and said, "Do not be afraid, for I know that you seek Jesus who was crucified. He is not here, for he has risen, as he said" (Matt. 28.5-6).

Their gloom was turned to inexpressible joy. The angel told them to go back and tell the disciples. As they were on their way, they met up with Jesus himself. So the women hurried away from the tomb, afraid, yet filled with joy, and ran to tell his disciples. Their three days of Dead Vision had been resurrected to new life along with Jesus himself.

Even when it seems that vision is dead, if it is God's will to continue, he will revive it in his time and in his way. God is in the business of Renewed Vision for those who attempt the Heroic Venture.

Questions for Discussion

1. With which biblical character did you most relate in this chapter? Why?
2. Describe a time when you experienced Renewed Vision when you thought your vision was dead.
3. When you felt your vision was dead, how did you maintain the faith to keep going?
4. Joshua wandered in the desert for forty years before he received Renewed Vision. How long are you willing to wait to see your vision renewed?

5. Hebrews 12.11 says, "For the moment all discipline seems painful rather than pleasant, but later it yields the peaceful fruit of righteousness to those who have been trained by it." How does this verse relate to the stories in this chapter?

Notes

[1] Bill Gothard. 1979. *Basic Seminar Textbook*. Oak Brook, IL: Institute for Basic Youth Conflicts, page 149-150.

Nagging Discouragement

Then the people of the land discouraged the people of Judah and made them afraid to build. ~ Ezra 4.4

September 1805

With the expedition united once more, their work was cut out for them. They had found the source of the Missouri but still had to cross the mountains and were dependent on the Shoshone guides to help them.

As they started on the perilous climb on September 11, 1805, they were nearly out of food. The route went through thickets on rocky hillsides where the horses were in constant danger of falling. In fact, the horses did frequently fall. Several times these falls appeared that they would result in certain death to the horses, but to the party's amazement, the horses got up with minimal injury. Ahead of them were the snow-covered Bitterroot Mountains, the most terrible the men had ever seen. According to the Shoshones, it would take at least six days to cross.

September 16 was the worst day of the expedition so far. Eight inches of snow fell. Clark said he had never been so wet and cold in every part of his body. The horses and men were near starvation, so some of the horses were killed for food. Spirits were low and the men were approaching their limits of physical endurance. Several of the men were sick with dysentery, yet retreat was unthinkable. They would rather die than quit. Besides, a five-day journey back was impossible.

Killing more horses would mean abandoning most of the provisions, so it was decided that Clark should take six hunters ahead to find food.

After six miles, Lewis reached a ridge, and to his inexpressible joy, saw a large prairie descending to the west. The sight greatly revived their spirits. The next day Lewis found food that Clark had left for them. With the party's strength renewed, Lewis ordered an eleven-day forced march over 160 miles of rough terrain before reaching the lodges of the Nez Perce.

They had conquered the Rockies, thanks to outstanding leadership, the disciplined perseverance of the men, and the skill of their Shoshone guides. During this ordeal, the Corps of Discovery did not sulk, lash out at their leaders, or insist on retreat. They had formed into a unit committed to the success of the enterprise.

Twisted Hair was chief of the Nez Perce. He told the expedition they were only a few weeks from the ocean. The captains had learned that Indian estimates were optimistic (or Indians were able to travel much faster), so they listened cautiously to the report.

During their visit with the Nez Perce, several men were sick with complaints of heaviness and bowel problems. They had eaten a boiled root that filled them with so much gas that they could scarcely breathe. For twelve days they continued to be sick, becoming feeble and emaciated. It would have been easy for the Nez Perce to kill them and steal their priceless goods.

In fact, Nez Perce oral history indicates the Indians did consider killing them but they were talked out of it by a woman named Watkuweis. Years before, she had been captured by the Blackfeet Indians and sold into slavery. Watkuweis maintained that the white traders she met had treated her better than the Blackfeet Indians, and urged Nez Perce mercy for the white man's expedition.

In a male-dominated world, this was the third time a woman had saved the expedition: Sacagawea, who rescued the supplies on the Missouri River, Jumping Fish, who accompanied Lewis to Chief Cameahwait, and now Watkuweis.

FIRST, THE vision was dead. Then it was renewed. The Corps of Discovery had fought through a number of grueling physical challenges. The trek through the mountains was difficult beyond description. The men were sick and vulnerable. Only the kindness of strangers kept them alive.

Discouragement is a persistent enemy. When facing emotional letdowns, one after another, it is tempting to give up. In the Heroic Venture, it is vital to persevere through Nagging Discouragement.

Perseverance

There are very few details about Noah's construction project, but the fact that it took 120 years to complete the ark according to God's design suggests its massive scope. No one can imagine what it would take to persevere for 120 years. Perhaps it was tedious at times. Maybe it was embarrassing to build a large boat on dry land. It certainly must have been difficult to collect the earth's animals into the ark. Perhaps there were those who opposed him, or maybe he got frustrated at times. Noah is the picture of perseverance in the face of Nagging Discouragement.

Doubt

God knew Gideon's tendency to doubt and second-guess and knew that Gideon would need more encouragement than most. As Gideon prepared his reduced army for battle, the Midianites were camped in the valley below. During the night, the Lord said to Gideon:

> Arise, go down against the camp, for I have given it into your hand. But if you are afraid to go down, go down to the camp with Purah your servant. And you shall hear what they say, and afterward your hands shall be strengthened to go down against the camp.
>
> ~ Judges 7.9-11

Gideon immediately took advantage of this opportunity, sneaking down to the outposts where the Midianites, Amalekites, and their allies were "like locusts in abundance." Just as Gideon arrived, he overheard a man explaining a dream to a fellow soldier. He said, "A cake of barley bread tumbled into the camp of Midian and came to the tent and struck it so that it fell and turned it upside down, so that the tent lay flat." The fellow soldier interpreted the dream, saying, "This is no other than the sword of Gideon the son of Joash, a man of Israel; God has given into his hand Midian and all the camp" (Judg. 7.12-14).

When Gideon heard the dream, he received the strength he needed. Filled with boldness, he thanked God and returned to the camp to rouse his army, saying, "Arise, for the Lord has given the host of Midian into your hand" (Judg. 7.15). Dividing the troops into three companies, he sent them to surround the enemy camp. They blew their trumpets, raised a racket by breaking jars, and shouted, "A sword for the Lord and for Gideon!" (v. 20). In response, the Midianites ran, crying out in fear as they fled and turned on each other with their swords. Not one of the three hundred Israelites needed to raise a weapon against the enemy.

Annoying Distractions

Nehemiah led the people to work on the wall despite opposition from Sanballat and Tobiah. He armed the people so they could serve "as guards by night and workmen by day" (Neh. 4.22, NIV). When the Jewish brothers were subjecting the people to unreasonable taxation, Nehemiah confronted them. He kept the people moving toward the vision. He rebuilt the wall without a gap left in it. As he was preparing to set the doors and gates, Sanballat and his cronies appeared again.

Nehemiah received a message inviting him to a meeting. Knowing it was a plot, he replied via messengers saying, "I am doing a great work and I cannot come down" (Neh. 6.3). This process was repeated four times. Nehemiah responded the same way each time. The fifth time, Sanballat and Geshem accused Nehemiah of planning a revolt and threatened to tell the king of Nehemiah's supposed disloyalty.

Aware that it was another deception to discourage the people, Nehemiah did not fall into their trap. He sent a terse refusal and prayed, "Now, O God, strengthen my hands" (6.9). He would not be distracted by Nagging Discouragement and relied on God to strengthen him. But the annoying distractions were not over.

Not long after this, another attempt to weaken the workers emerged, this time from Shemaiah, who urged a closed-door meeting with Nehemiah in the temple. Shemaiah used the pretense that he was trying to save Nehemiah from an assassination plot. Sensing the deception, Nehemiah refused to be involved. He realized Sanballat had hired him "to intimidate me so that I would commit a sin by doing this, and then they would give me a bad name to discredit me" (6.13, NIV). Nehemiah kept going despite persistent badgering.

Giving in to Nagging

Unlike Nehemiah, Zerubbabel fell victim to Nagging Discouragement. He and Jeshua were successfully rebuilding the temple, under orders from King Cyrus, when they uncovered a plot of their enemies to destroy their work. Pretending to be allies, they asked to join the team. When Zerubbabel refused their request, a new threat emerged:

> Then the people of the land discouraged the people of Judah and made them afraid to build and bribed counselors against them to frustrate their purpose, all the days of Cyrus king of Persia, even until the reign of Darius king of Persia.
>
> ~ Ezra 4.4-5

After four years of work and opposition, the people stopped working on the temple, leaving it unfinished. "The work on the house of God in Jerusalem came to a standstill" (4.24, NIV).

Delilah worked hard to get Samson to reveal the source of his strength. In fact, after many failed attempts, Delilah said, "You have mocked me these three times, and you have not told me where you great strength lies" (Judg. 16.15). The author of Judges said, "with such nagging she prodded him day after day" (16.16, NIV) until Samson could not take it any more. Delilah's nagging wore Samson down until he finally gave up and told her everything. Delilah sent word to her Philistine co-conspirators and Samson was quickly imprisoned. Samson was another leader who gave in to Nagging Discouragement.

It is easy to get discouraged in the Heroic Venture, but Paul said, "Let us not grow weary of doing good, for in due season we will reap, if we do not give up" (Gal. 6.9). In their Heroic Ventures, Nehemiah, Noah, and Gideon lived out this principle, while Nagging Discouragement got the better of Samson and Zerubbabel.

Questions for Discussion

1. What are some ways you get discouraged?
2. If you face Dead Vision, but then persevere to Renewed Vision, how should you respond if you then face a new set of discouraging events?
3. What are some of the forms of discouragement experienced by the biblical characters in this chapter? How did they handle that discouragement?
4. What do you think would have happened if Noah, Gideon, and Nehemiah had given in to Nagging Discouragement? How would their lives have been different? What would have happened in history?
5. How would history have changed if Zerubbabel and Samson had not given in to Nagging Discouragement?

Daring Decisions

*David ran quickly toward the battle line to meet the Philistine.
And David put his hand in his bag and took out a stone and
slung it and struck the Philistine on his forehead.*

~ 1 Samuel 17.48-49

October - November 1805

The Corps of Discovery developed a friendship with the Nez
Perce, who proved to be hospitable, and asked the party to stay
longer. Lewis was torn between his desire to keep moving and
the goal of bringing the Nez Perce into the American sphere of
diplomacy. The captains decided they would stay for a longer
visit during their return trip in the spring of 1806.

The Nez Perce showed them how to build burned-out canoes.
When they were finished, the party was off once again. On
October 6, 1805, the expedition swept on toward the junction
of the Snake and Columbia Rivers in present-day Washington,
then on to the Columbian plain. The barren landscape sharply
contrasted the wooded mountains they recently left behind. As
they proceeded, they encountered a number of rapids that
seemed too dangerous to travel.

Their canoes were cumbersome and could easily be swamped,
springing leaks on many occasions. Even though the party faced
dangerous rapids, sometimes as many as fifteen times per day,

the men pressed the captains to run the rapids rather than waste time making portages. The Shoshone guide, "Old Toby," was so frightened by their actions that he left in the night without receiving his pay.

At one point they reached a twenty-foot drop that had to be portaged. They hired local Indians and horses to help with the heavier items and received guidance on how to maneuver the river downstream.

When they reached a set of falls (now known as The Dalles, east of Portland, Oregon), Clark was appalled by the horrid appearance of this "agitated gut-swelling water, boiling and whirling in every direction." In modern terms it was a Class V rapid, meaning even a modern canoe, designed for rapids, could not survive it. The captains selected the priority items to be carried on land such as journals, rifles, and scientific instruments. Then they proceeded to attempt to run The Dalles in their canoes.

The native tribes, who were expert canoeists, came to the banks of the river by the hundreds to watch the foolish white men drown themselves. The Indians were also ready to collect the expedition's equipment and supplies after their demise. But to the astonishment of the onlookers, the travelers survived without incident. Later, they repeated this feat at Long Narrows, again with a large number of Indian spectators watching them defy the odds.

As they made their way down the Columbia, the Corps of Discovery encountered the Chinook, Tillamook, and Clatsop tribes. They were not as warlike as the plains Indians, but the Chinooks were constantly stealing from the expedition. The team's supplies were limited, so any loss was significant. On a number of occasions, the men had to be restrained from violence because of the aggravation caused by the petty theft. The party was not looking forward to a winter with these tribes after such a warm friendship with the Nez Perce and Mandans.

On November 2, they reached western territory that had been previously mapped by other explorers. Now the maps of east and west could come together for the first time. They were making good progress every day and, on November 7, sighted what they thought was the Pacific Ocean.

A GOOD leader recognizes the opportune time to take courageous action. Lewis and Clark were willing to face Class V rapids to keep on schedule to reach the Pacific Ocean. The Bible gives examples of leaders making bold and Daring Decisions to keep the project moving.

Esther

Queen Esther found out about Haman's plan to extinguish the Jews. When Mordecai asked her to intercede on behalf of the Jews, she knew such a plan would be risky. Her predecessor, Queen Vashti, had recently been deposed. Queens were not above being replaced. But Mordecai made it clear that Esther would not be exempt from Haman's execution. She was between a rock and a hard place. When she asked Mordecai to organize prayer for her, she knew her life was in danger when she said, "I will go to the king, though it is against the law, and if I perish, I perish" (Esther 4.16). She was ready to die for her mission.

David

Goliath stood with the Philistine army on one hill, facing the Israelites on another. For forty days in a row, Goliath came out every morning to defy the ranks of Israel and challenge them to a one-on-one fight. Into the scene walked David, wandering innocently into camp to deliver bread to his brothers in the army. Shortly after he arrived, the daily Goliath spectacle began. David saw what was happening and overheard talk about the reward for the one who would fight Goliath. Word got to King Saul that there was a volunteer, and David was quickly brought to the king's tent to be interviewed.

David convinced Saul that he was up to the task, and with sling in hand, chose five smooth stones from the stream. Seeing David's youth, Goliath mocked David saying, "Come to me, and I will give your flesh to the birds of the air and to the beasts of the field" (1 Sam. 17.44). Rather than shrinking back in fear, David responded in kind.

> This day the Lord will deliver you into my hand, and I will strike you down and cut off your head. And I will give the dead bodies of the host of the

Philistines this day to the birds of the air and to the wild beasts of the earth, that all the earth may know that there is a God in Israel.

~ 1 Samuel 17.46

As the enemy drew closer to attack, David executed his plan. Running quickly toward the battle line, David reached into his bag, loaded his weapon and connected, dropping Goliath unconscious (17.48). David showed incredible faith and daring.

Samson

The people of Judah wanted to appease their Philistine oppressors, so they sought out Samson to hand him over to the enemy. But Samson was in hiding. When they finally found him, they bound him with ropes. As he was led away, the Spirit of God came upon him and he struck down one thousand Philistines with the jawbone of a donkey (Judg. 15.14-18). Samson showed his passion for defeating the Philistines when his fellow Israelites were prepared to give in.

Peter

Five years after the death and resurrection of Jesus, the Gentiles had not yet received the Gospel, and were expected to become Jews before becoming Christians. A diligent Jew was expected to keep the dietary laws and refrain from association with Gentiles. Yet the Church was growing, Paul had been converted, the Gospel was being preached, and miracles were taking place in Jesus' name.

Peter raised Tabitha from the dead, which created a revival in Joppa, causing Peter to stay there for an extended time.

Cornelius, a God-fearing Gentile living thirty miles away in Caesarea, received a vision instructing him to invite Peter to come to his home. At the same moment Peter was praying on a rooftop in Joppa, two of Cornelius' servants were on their way to ask Peter to come to a Gentile home, a clear violation of Jewish custom.

Peter was rash and impulsive by nature, but it took some coaxing from God to convince him to go to a Gentile's home to deliver the Gospel message. Peter knew he would be severely criticized by his fellow Jews for breaking such a long-standing rule of Jewish culture. Cornelius' belief in the message led to his household receiving the Holy Spirit, launching a broad expansion of the Church in the world. Peter took a brazen step of faith that made the Great Commission possible, even though he needed to be nudged along.

Philip

Sometimes a daring response requires leaving a safe, fruitful ministry to start something new and unknown. Philip was among the original deacons in the Jerusalem church. After the stoning of Stephen, Philip went to a city in Samaria to preach the Gospel, and was experiencing an amazing response, with miraculous signs that drew attention to his message. Evil spirits were being driven out, and people were healed. Even a leading sorcerer was baptized. So much was happening in Samaria that leading apostles, Peter and John, were sent there as reinforcements to support Philip's ministry. "There was much joy in that city" (Acts 8.8).

While Philip was enjoying such a great response in Samaria, an angel abruptly instructed him to leave Samaria and go to the desert road from Jerusalem to Gaza, about one hundred miles away. He was asked to leave a thriving ministry, full of miracles and good fruit, in order to walk alone on a desert road for some unknown reason.

Along the way he met an Ethiopian official in charge of the queen's treasury, reading the prophet Isaiah. God had prepared the situation for just the right moment. The official asked Philip to explain the passage, and upon receiving the Good News, the Ethiopian asked to be baptized at the side of the road. When they came out of the water, Philip was miraculously whisked twenty miles away to the city of Azotus.

Philip was willing to listen to the guidance of the Holy Spirit, even without a full explanation. Because he was open to leave a flourishing work, his obedience resulted in the Gospel being spread to Ethiopia. Simple obedience sometimes requires leaving the comfort of the familiar.

Jesus

Daring Decisions involve a willingness to confront others. Jesus was often hounded by Jewish leaders who wanted to accuse him, catching him in an awkward moment. Jesus was angry because they cared more about their reputations than they cared about the people.

One Sabbath day Jesus went into a synagogue and saw a man with a shriveled hand. The Jewish leaders watched closely to see if Jesus would break the Sabbath by healing the man. Recognizing their motives, Jesus provoked the situation by telling the man to stand up in front of everyone. Then he irritated the Jewish leaders further by asking, "Is it lawful on the Sabbath to do good or to do harm, to save life or to kill?" (Mark 3.4). Angry and distressed by their hard hearts, Jesus confronted them by telling the man, "Stretch out your hand" (3.5). As he did, the man's hand was completely restored.

Jesus' passion to destroy the devil's work led him to fight hard against those who would trivialize the suffering of others. His zeal incited the Pharisee's wrath. From then on, they began to plot how they might kill Jesus.

Paul
Even under house arrest in Rome, Paul was passionate about sharing the Good News, "proclaiming the kingdom of God and teaching about the Lord Jesus Christ with all boldness and without hindrance" (Acts 28.31).

Daring Decisions can involve unpleasant consequences, yet they are an essential part of the Heroic Venture. "The wicked flee when no one pursues, but the righteous are bold as a lion" (Prov. 28.1).

Questions for Discussion

1. How did the biblical project leaders show boldness?
2. Daring Decisions come in many forms. How did Philip show boldness?
3. Give some examples for why boldness is needed to keep a project moving.
4. Do you see yourself as a bold person by nature? Why or why not? Give examples.
5. If you were to counsel someone who is careful by nature, how would you explain how to exercise boldness at the appropriate time?

Patient Waiting

And thus Abraham, having patiently waited,
obtained the promise. ~ Hebrews 6.15

November 1805 - April 1806

On November 10, 1805, the expedition reached a campsite
but was unable to move forward or retreat because of a rain-
storm that trapped them for eleven days. Fires were hard to
start. Their bedding was soggy all night long. Their clothes were
nearly rotted away. They looked more like survivors from a ship-
wreck than the triumphant members of the Corps of Discovery.
On November 22, the wind increased with such violence that it
threw immense waves over the banks and overwhelmed the
party. Clark said, "O how horrible is the day."

Lewis had not made a journal entry since September. Historians
wonder if Lewis was experiencing the depression that caused
Jefferson concern. It could have been that Lewis was discouraged about the report he had to give Jefferson. The rigors of
the Columbia's falls only reinforced that there was no easy
water route across the continent. Lewis may have also been
despondent about the return voyage, knowing what it would
take to get back home.

Whatever Lewis may have been going through is purely
speculation. But if he did suffer from depression, which is

widely believed, it was a special mark of heroism that he could lead the project under such conditions. It is even more remarkable when he may have been an alcoholic who had not had liquor for four months. He had quit "cold turkey" while leading a complex and dangerous mission across an unknown frontier.

Despite the silence of his journals, Lewis had a passion to press on. The journey would be a failure if he could not get the journals back to Jefferson. The water route was important, but the scientific discoveries were now the primary object of his work. He had to get that information back to his boss.

By November 27, the expedition needed to set up winter camp, but they were so immobilized by the weather that they had to be rescued by the Clatsop Indians. The Clatsops gave them roots and fish and suggested alternative places to set up their winter home. The captains had to choose a location based on three priorities. They needed to be close to game to provide food; near the ocean to spot a possible passing ship (for supplies); and close to a convenient place to refine salt from the ocean.

Typically the captains made the decisions, but this time they let everyone participate in a vote. Even Sacagawea (a non-citizen woman) and York (a slave) participated. It was the first recorded time in American history that an Indian woman and a Black man were given the right to vote. The group decided on a forested area between the Columbia and the Pacific and called it Fort Clatsop, in honor of their new Indian neighbors.

The party spent the winter making salt and new clothes, repairing equipment, and recovering from illness. Throughout the winter, it rained constantly, and their camp was infested with fleas. The men were constantly ill with fevers and influenza, and they were almost broke. The captains were unable to make celestial observations because of the consistent cloud cover. It was difficult to be patient. They were eager to get back on their way.

Clark worked on his map, connecting the previously unknown section from Mandan to Clatsop. This map was an invaluable contribution to the world's knowledge. But for the other members of the party, the winter at Clatsop was unbelievably dull. On Christmas morning everyone exchanged presents, such as they were, which only made them more homesick. No ships ever passed by to bring them supplies. Clatsop became more like a prison than a winter home.

Excitement was rare. One day a whale beached on the shore. Sacagawea was excited to see the ocean, the first Shoshone to do so. The beached whale provided valuable blubber that the expedition could use in trade on the way home.

Meanwhile, the Spanish had heard about the expedition and were afraid the Corps of Discovery was sent to raid their gold and silver mines. So the Spanish sent their own expeditions to find them and cut them off. Four parties were sent over two years, but they never connected with Lewis and Clark. Jefferson had also sent out expeditions to other areas of the continent, but none was successful. All returned home early without completing their missions.

As the party prepared to leave Clatsop to head home, the captains received reports that salmon was scarce and tribes were starving upriver. But they could not afford to wait too long and get caught for another winter before reaching St. Louis. On April 7, 1806, the Corps of Discovery finally set out from Clatsop. Compared to their plentiful supplies at Mandan, they departed with almost nothing.

As they passed up river they continued to be victimized by rampant petty theft from the Indians. Tempers were running high. Anything left unguarded, even for a moment, was gone. Guards had to be assigned to watch the baggage. When Lewis' dog was stolen, his pent-up anger turned into full-blown rage. He sent out a team to find the dog and shoot the thieves, if needed. The party was at the edge of serious violence. Giving in to their frustration would not only ruin relationships with the people they were trying to befriend, but also put the whole expedition in danger. The dog was quickly found and Lewis calmed himself to reconcile with the chief whose people had taken the dog.

Along the way, more items continued to be stolen. After a number of incidents, an Indian was caught stealing, raising Lewis' wrath again. This time, Lewis beat the thief, threw him out of camp, and threatened to light his home on fire. But before he took such drastic action, Lewis composed himself and moved on. Patience was running thin.

On April 24, Chief Yellept of the Wallawallas told Lewis about a shortcut home that would shave 80 miles off their previous route. Two teenage Wallawallas came into camp with a steel trap the party had left behind, an act of integrity unseen in the thieving tribes down river. The party was relieved to be back with friends, who were described as the "most hospitable, honest, and sincere people that we have met with in our voyage." Waiting at Fort Clatsop had been agonizing, but now they were among friends and on their way home.

But as they moved on, their troubles were not over. On May 1, the weather was miserable, and the captains divided the last portion of food. There was nothing left to eat. The party was on the brink of starvation.

FOR MANY, the waiting at Fort Clatsop had been the worst part of the journey. Waiting can be a terribly difficult part of the Heroic Venture. With a clear vision from the Lord, the ministry leader's natural desire is to be busy in pursuit of that vision. But sometimes waiting is required, letting God do things behind the scenes. While Daring Decisions are often the right choice, there are many occasions when the wise thing is to wait and let things develop.

Abraham waited twenty-five years for his promise to be fulfilled. He was seventy-five when God told him he would be the father of a great nation (Gen. 12.1) and one hundred when Isaac was born. Abraham is the picture of Patient Waiting.

A cake takes time to bake. There is nothing that can be done to speed the baking process.

Esther

As Esther committed to approach the king, her first order of business was to dedicate herself to three days of prayer and fasting, and requested her maids, friends, and family to do the same.

Then, when she had opportunity to see the king, she did not directly address the issue, but invited the king and Haman to a banquet that day. At the banquet, the king knew there was something deeper on her mind and inquired about it. Esther, once again, was led to wait. She asked the king to come to another banquet the next day, at which time she would make her request known to the king.

God used this time of waiting, in dramatic fashion, to set up the rescue of the Jews. That night, the king could not sleep and ordered a book of chronicles to be read to him. Of all the stories that could be selected, the story of Mordecai's prevention of an assassination plot was chosen. Through this reading, the king found that Mordecai had never been properly honored for this courageous service.

The king knew nothing about Esther's family connection with, nor Haman's bitter resentment toward, Mordecai. It was God's providence that Haman would walk in just as the king was ready to praise Mordecai. The king said, "What should be done to the man whom the king delights to honor?" (Esther 6.6). Thinking King Xerxes was referring to him, Haman responded in lavish detail, including the placement of a royal robe and a crown, then a processional through the city with announcements of "Thus shall it be done to the man whom the king delights to honor" (6.9).

The king was thrilled with his suggestions, but Haman was shocked and humiliated at the news that Mordecai would be the recipient instead of Haman. After Haman sheepishly ushered Mordecai through the city, Haman was immediately delivered to Esther's second banquet.

The king asked Esther again about the nature of her request. Now the time was right. Esther's Patient Waiting had prepared the king, and Haman, for the occasion.

Esther revealed that her people, the Jews, had been sold to destruction, slaughter, and annihilation. The king was enraged and asked who would do such a thing. Esther said "A foe and enemy! This wicked Haman!" (7.6). In despair, Haman pleaded with Esther for his life. But the king had Haman hanged on the very same gallows that was built for Mordecai. Waiting on the Lord was the wise choice. God vindicated Mordecai and brought justice to Haman.

Nehemiah

When Nehemiah heard the news about Jerusalem's devastation, he was heartbroken. But he did not rush to action. He prayed, fasted, planned, and waited for an opportunity to act. It was four months before he had opportunity to mention anything to the king. Prayer is an important part of Patient Waiting.

Diplomatic Waiting

Jephthah was selected as judge and deliverer when the Ammonites came against Israel. Rather than rush into battle, Jephthah was willing to wait for a diplomatic solution. He wrote the king of Ammon, asking for the reason for their invasion. After receiving the correspondence, Jephthah crafted a careful response to attempt a peaceful solution. After a period of waiting without an answer, the Spirit of the Lord came upon Jephthah, who attacked and devastated Ammon's army (Judg. 11.11-33).

God's Patience

God had determined to wipe out the people on earth, saving only Noah's family. He was willing to wait many years for the people of the day to repent. He is "slow to anger, and abounding in steadfast love and faithfulness" (Exod. 34.6). "God waited patiently in the days of Noah while the ark was being built" (1 Pet. 3.20, NIV).

Jonah spent three days and three nights in the belly of a great fish. God used this event to bring Jonah to a willingness to accept his Nineveh assignment. This time of waiting contributed to Jonah's repentance. When Jonah was ready to obey, God released him by having the fish vomit him onto dry land.

The Strategic Moment

Jesus heard his friend Lazarus was sick in Bethany, but he waited two days before going there. By the time Jesus arrived, Lazarus had been dead for four days. It was the Father's will that Lazarus would be raised from the dead at the proper time and place. Only two miles from Jerusalem, this news would travel quickly to those who were wanting to arrest and kill Jesus. Such a dramatic miracle alarmed the Jewish leaders and set into motion the events leading to Jesus' crucifixion (John 11.1-48). Jesus was willing to wait patiently for the right strategic moment, even when his dear friend's life was involved.

Visionary leaders may find it difficult to wait. However, even when plans are delayed, it is important to display Patient Waiting, knowing that God is at work behind the scenes in the Heroic Venture.

Questions for Discussion

1. Why was the winter at Clatsop (1805-06) more difficult than the winter at Mandan (1804-1805)?

179

2. How do you think Abraham, Nehemiah, Esther, and Jephthah handled their time of waiting?
3. Explain why patience is important in keeping a project moving.
4. Are you a patient person by nature? Is it easier for you to make Daring Decisions or exhibit Patient Waiting? Give examples.
5. If you were to counsel someone who is impatient by nature, how would you explain how to exercise patience at the appropriate time?

Prudent Counsel

*Rise, take the child and his mother, and flee to Egypt,
and remain there until I tell you.* ~ Matthew 2.13

May - June 1806

On May 4, 1806, after three days without food, the party
encountered a band of Nez Perce who sold them some roots to
eat, saving them from starvation. They were rescued from
extinction once again.

The Indians took them back to Chief Twisted Hair who was
keeping their horses over the winter. The captains found
Twisted Hair in conflict with another tribal chief. Lewis and
Clark were able to mediate a peaceful reconciliation, which
only strengthened the bonds of trust and friendship between
the Nez Perce and Corps of Discovery.

The previous year, Clark had treated an old man's knee, so
while they were gone, Clark's reputation as a healer had grown
with the Nez Perce. When Clark arrived in the village, he was
surprised to be in great demand as a doctor for the Indians in
distress. Since his heat treatments proved successful, his medical services became an important means of trading for goods
and supplies, just as the battle axes had been at Mandan. The
Nez Perce offered the captains as many horses as they needed,
which was welcome news.

The mountains ahead were covered with snow, so the Nez Perce counseled them against making passage until June. Morale sank at this news. They would have to stay three more weeks, and they were eager to keep moving. They had nothing to eat except dried fish, roots, and an occasional elk.

To increase morale, athletic contests were held between the Corps of Discovery and the Nez Perce Indians. Spectators from each culture came out to cheer them on. The party enjoyed their time with the tribe and a genuine friendship developed. But the party was tense, ready to vault over the mountains.

The snowfall that year was greater than normal and the Indians warned it could be into July before the expedition could depart. A premature migration could result in forcing the horses to go without food for three days. But the Indians' advice did not keep the party from setting out. By June 9, the party was elated with the prospect of moving toward home. Just before the Corps of Discovery left, the Nez Perce promised to send guides to meet up with them, despite the fact that the captains were not following Nez Perce counsel.

The party reached the same site where they almost died eating gas-inducing roots the year before. By now they had become accustomed to the roots and ate them without incident. But they were concerned because the Nez Perce guides did not show up. The captains decided to take a long march instead of waiting. This was a big risk, but Lewis felt the need to keep moving.

Within four hours, they faced harsh winter conditions. They were six days away from safety, assuming they did not get lost along the way. If they did get lost, their horses would die and they would risk the loss of the journals and instruments that were essential to their mission. The captains realized the foolishness of their decision and turned back to get a guide while the horses were still strong. On June 17, 1806, for the first time in the expedition, they were making a retreat, but for good reason.

They sent a small group to find the Nez Perce while the rest of the party waited for them. On the third day of waiting, just as they considered going on without them, the rest of the group appeared with the guides.

With the guides leading the way, the expedition was back on the road by June 24. On June 27, they reached an elevated spot with an extensive view of the mountains, which filled them with awe, dread, and great respect for the Indian guides. It seemed impossible to have escaped without their assistance. The trail was covered with ten feet of snow, heavily wooded, and often dangerous. Lewis' horse slipped, and Lewis slid forty feet toward his death, but was saved as he grabbed a branch to stop himself.

On June 30, they safely reached camp at a place they called "Traveler's Rest." It was time to say a sad goodbye to their friends, the Nez Perce. It was the Indians who fed them when they were hungry, provided fuel when they were cold, gave them horses and guides, and offered the captains Prudent

Counsel. The two peoples had shared experiences that drew them together. The Nez Perce could not hide their anxiety for their new friends. They were confident the Plains Indians would kill the party before they reached home.

THE NEZ PERCE had become dear friends to the Corps of Discovery, which caused the Indians to give heartfelt advice to preserve their lives. Although the expedition wanted to press ahead, they realized that the Nez Perce were giving Prudent Counsel. It was painful to hear, but their trust and affection helped the captains consider their advice. "Oil and perfume make the heart glad, and the sweetness of a friend comes from his earnest counsel" (Prov. 27.9). "Faithful are the wounds of a friend" (Prov. 27.6).

Listening to Prudent Counsel can help accomplish the vision. It can also save lives. Wisdom and passion come together when leaders pay attention to advice. "Without counsel plans fail" (Prov. 15.22). Consider some biblical examples where God provided Prudent Counsel.

Joseph and Mary

An angel appeared to Joseph in a dream, instructing him to move his young family to Egypt until further notice (Matt. 2.13-15). Herod was preparing to kill baby Jesus. It was the second recorded time that Joseph received instruction through dreams (Matt. 1.20). Joseph had learned to trust God's Prudent Counsel through his dreams.

The Rebuilding of the Temple

Zerubbabel, and the people who joined him in rebuilding the temple, had become so discouraged after four years of persistent opposition, that their work came to a complete halt. For ten years, the temple sat unfinished while the people went on with their lives. Then, God sent two prophets, Haggai and Zechariah, to counsel and encourage Zerubbabel.

Haggai said, "Is it a time for you yourselves to dwell in your paneled houses, while this house lies in ruins?" (Hag. 1.4). "Go up to the hills and bring wood and build the house, that I may take pleasure in it and that I may be glorified, says the Lord" (Hag. 1.8). He pointed to recent crop conditions as evidence that God was withholding blessing due to inattention to the temple project. Zerubbabel, Jeshua, and the people obeyed the word of the Lord and got back to work.

Haggai encouraged them further with the Lord's message, "Be strong, all you people of the land, declares the Lord. Work, for I am with you, declares the Lord of hosts, according to the covenant that I made with you when you came out of Egypt. My Spirit remains in your midst. Fear not" (Hag. 2.4-5). The people were excited to resume the work.

Meanwhile, as the construction started, Zerubbabel's adversaries resumed their resistance to the project. The governor and his associates went to Zerubbabel and said, "Who gave you a decree to build this house and to finish this structure? . . . What are the names of the men who are building this building?" (Ezra 5.3-4). The leaders explained that King Cyrus had given authority to rebuild the temple sixteen years earlier, before the present King Darius had taken the throne.

In spite of this antagonism, the people kept building because "The eye of their God was on the elders of the Jews" (Ezra 5.5). The governor wrote a letter to King Darius to settle the dispute. After receiving their letter, Darius ordered the matter to be properly researched. A scroll was found that corroborated Zerubbabel's story, so Darius issued a new decree, giving authority to rebuild the temple, financed by the royal treasury. The governor was given clear orders not to interfere with the project, at the risk of a violent and unpleasant death.

Zechariah and Haggai continued to encourage the people. For those who had seen the glory of the previous temple, God inspired them by saying:

> Yet once more, in a little while, I will shake the heavens and the earth and the sea and the dry land. And I will shake all nations, so that the treasures of all nations shall come in, and I will fill this house with glory, says the Lord of hosts. The silver is mine, and the gold is mine, declares the Lord of

hosts. The latter glory of this house shall be greater than the former.

~ Haggai 2.6-9

Zechariah's prophecies foretold the conquering Messiah King. There would be a day of the Lord when the Messiah would come to defeat his enemies and rescue his people. These prophecies motivated the people, knowing there were higher stakes than their own personal comfort and ambitions. They were part of the reconstruction of the temple that Messiah himself would visit.

Zechariah said:

> Rejoice greatly, O daughter of Zion! Shout aloud, O daughter of Jerusalem! behold, your king is coming to you; righteous and having salvation is he, humble and mounted on a donkey, on a colt, the foal of a donkey.
>
> ~ Zechariah 9.9

Finally, God had a personal message for Zerubbabel. God spoke through Haggai, saying:

> Speak to Zerubbabel, governor of Judah, saying, I am about to shake the heavens and the earth, and to overthrow the throne of kingdoms. I am about to destroy the strength of the kingdoms of the nations, and overthrow the chariots and their riders. And the horses and their riders shall go down, every one by the sword of his brother. On that day, declares

the Lord of hosts, I will take you, O Zerubbabel my servant, the son of Shealtiel, declares the Lord, and make you like a signet ring, for I have chosen you.

~ Haggai 2.21-23

God revealed Zerubbabel's participation in the lineage of Jesus (see Matt. 1.12), providing him motivation to lead the people with confidence.

Haggai and Zechariah were tremendous sources of Prudent Counsel. Without them, the temple may not have been rebuilt.

It is important for leaders to listen to Prudent Counsel. If a leader chooses not to listen, the results can be damaging to the Heroic Venture. "The way of a fool is right in his own eyes, but a wise man listens to advice" (Prov. 12.15).

Questions for Discussion

1. Why were Lewis and Clark open to the counsel of the Nez Perce?
2. What would have happened if they had ignored the counsel of the Nez Perce?
3. What role did Haggai and Zechariah have in God's plan?
4. Explain the meaning of Proverbs 27.6: "Wounds from a friend can be trusted."

5. Why is it important to seek counsel when making decisions about your project?

Tempting Distractions

Jehoash said to the priests, "All the money of the holy things that is brought into the house of the Lord . . . let the priests take . . . and let them repair the house wherever any need of repairs is discovered." But by the twenty-third year of King Jehoash, the priests had made no repairs on the house."

~ 2 Kings 12.4-6

June - August 1806

On June 30, 1806, Lewis and Clark had escaped much of the danger and unknown and were clearly on their way home. For the most part, they had completed their mission, but the captains still had a few more objectives. They wanted to provide Jefferson with an optimum land route across the continent. Lewis wanted to explore the northern boundary of the Louisiana Purchase (located at 49 degrees latitude). They also hoped to strike a trade deal with the Blackfeet Indians, whom they had not met on their trip west. So, on July 3, the captains split the expedition into five sub-parties, according to a plan they had devised during their winter at Clatsop.

Lewis would follow the Nez Perce shortcut to the Great Falls. Three of Lewis' group would stay there to prepare for the portage around the Falls. Lewis would take the remaining party north to ascend the Marias River.

A third group would proceed with Ordway to the head of the Jefferson River to pick up the supplies they had left the year before, then meet up with the Lewis party.

Clark would take the fourth group to explore the Yellowstone River and map the area until it connected with the Missouri. Then Clark would build canoes for the trip down the Missouri.

The fifth group was assigned to deliver a special letter to Hugh Heney, an important envoy, who was probably at the Mandan village. Lewis believed Heney could influence the Sioux to affiliate with the Americans instead of the advancing British.

For the first time they were dividing the party to pursue different objectives. This ambitious plan was exceedingly complex. Huge responsibilities were being given to sergeants and privates. The plan's success depended on precision timing, few unexpected problems, and extraordinary performance from the group.

They were one thousand miles from any outposts and destitute of trading materials. Split into five vulnerable groups in the western plains that were teeming with roving Indian war parties, they were heading straight into the territory of the Blackfeet, who were heavily armed with rifles. Any one of the groups would be easy to defeat.

On July 26, Lewis, flanked at a distance by Drouillard and the two Shields brothers, looked through his telescope. He was alarmed to see a band of Blackfeet Indians watching Drouillard from a distance.

Lewis slowly made his way toward the Indians who were then alarmed to see Lewis appear. The natives sent their horses into a frenzied circle, then a single rider broke from their pack and came full speed toward Lewis. Lewis dismounted and stood waiting for the Indian in hopes of displaying a peaceful posture.

Disarmed by Lewis' reaction, the Indian stopped one hundred yards away, wheeled the horse around and galloped back to the pack. Lewis' group assembled, now outnumbered nine to four.

The Indians then rode out and met Lewis' party, shook hands, and smoked a peace pipe. Lewis discovered that there was a British outpost only six days away, the British were firmly entrenched in that area, and they were rapidly moving south. This confirmed Jefferson's fears about the expansion of British influence in the region.

Lewis made an attempt to strike a better deal with the Blackfeet. He told them about his promise to sell rifles to the Nez Perce and Shoshones. This was a terrible political mistake since the Blackfeet were arch enemies of the Nez Perce and Shoshones. After twenty years of being the dominant bully on the block, the Blackfeet would now have to contend with warring nations having equal firepower.

The next morning, Lewis woke to the sound of Drouillard shouting that his gun had been stolen. Lewis reached for his rifle and it was gone also. Drawing his pistol from its holster, he saw an Indian running away with his rifle. Lewis ran at him, ordering him to lay down the rifle or be shot. The Indian laid the rifle down. Lewis' men collected their rifles, but not before killing a Blackfoot who had resisted.

The Indians were falling back while attempting to scatter Lewis' horses, which would leave the party stranded. The men prevented this and gave chase to the Indians. A warrior fired at Lewis, who felt the bullet fly over his head. He fired back at the Blackfeet, wounding one of them. Lewis decided to retreat before Blackfoot reinforcements arrived.

Their lives in danger, Lewis' party quickly loaded their horses and raced away without stopping until 2 a.m. After a few hours sleep, they were on their way again. When they met up with Ordway's party, they quickly explained the need for speed, put their baggage in the canoes, and released the horses.

Lewis' group reached the goods they had stashed the year before. Some items had rotted away, but most were in good working order.

During their retreat, Lewis found out the full story. Shields had slept during guard duty at the worst possible moment – right before dawn. This created a tempting opportunity for the Blackfeet. It was inexcusable to lay down a rifle while on duty, especially while camping with potential enemy combatants.

One would have thought after two years in the wilderness this kind of error would have been avoided.

Lewis was right to make efforts to get the rifles and horses back, but chasing the retreating Blackfeet was a mistake that could have been fatal. He left the camp unsecured and exposed himself to unnecessary harm.

A few days later, on August 11, Lewis and Private Cruzatte went elk hunting in the willows. As Lewis raised his rifle to shoot, he was hit in the rear by a rifle shot, which spun him around. Lewis yelled at Cruzatte but there was no response, so Lewis guessed it was an Indian attack. In an effort to rally the men, Lewis ran one hundred yards toward the boat and called them to arms. After struggling to get in the boat, he waited in terrible suspense for the rest of the party to return. Finally, after twenty minutes, the crew arrived. When the bullet was removed from Lewis' behind, it was an Army-issue bullet, proving that Cruzatte was the shooter. Lewis ordered the men to move on, their commander lying face down in the boat, in pain and humiliation.

WHILE THEIR motives were right, Lewis and Clark made a mistake by splitting up the party. In their attempt to find the best route across the continent, they put the entire mission at risk. They had become distracted from their primary aim. They were trying to accomplish too much.

Instead, they needed to stay focused on their priorities. Ministry leaders are also prone to lose focus.

Abraham

Tempting Distractions can come in the form of trying to do God's work in man's way. While Abraham showed great patience for twenty-five years, waiting for the promise to be fulfilled, he had a lapse in judgment and had a son named Ishmael through Sarah's maidservant, Hagar. Abraham was trying to fulfill God's promises in his own way. Although his motives were right, it was a bad idea that had lasting implications.

Once Isaac came along, Ishmael went from "the promised one" to a second-class citizen. When Ishmael showed resentment toward Isaac (Gen. 21.9), Sarah requested Ishmael's banishment. Abraham agreed, and it was only by God's intervention that Ishmael and Hagar survived. The bitterness of this rejection must have affected them. Decades later, the Ishmaelites were the ones who purchased Joseph and sold him into Egyptian slavery (Exod. 37.27) and the descendants of Ishmael continued to be hostile to God and his people (Ps. 83.6).

Samson

Samson was easily distracted from his responsibilities. Although he was set apart from birth as a Nazirite, assigned to "begin to save Israel from the hand of the Philistines" (Judg. 13.5), he continually confided in the wrong people and was controlled more by pleasure than obedience to his mission. Ironically, his Nazirite vow required abstaining from alcohol, yet he lived a reckless and indulgent lifestyle.

Samson made a silly bet with his Philistine in-laws, based on a riddle he challenged them to solve. His wife easily coaxed the riddle's answer from Samson. Later, he visited a prostitute that left him vulnerable to enemy capture. Then he lived with another Philistine woman (Delilah) who ended up serving as an enemy agent. Although Samson clearly squandered his great talents on practical jokes and foolish decisions, God used him to accomplish his mission. Despite falling to Tempting Distractions on many occasions, Samson showed enough faithfulness to be included in the hall of faith (Heb. 11.32). Samson's life is an example; avoid Tempting Distractions, but never be discouraged by failure to the point of giving up.

Jehoash

King Jehoash instructed his priests to "take, each from his donor, and let them repair the house wherever any need of repairs is discovered" (2 Kings 12.5). But twenty-three years went by and the priests still had not done the work they were assigned. When King Jehoash found out, he summoned the priests and made them finish the project.

Jehoash gave the assignment, but got distracted and never checked on the work. It is easy to get caught up in good activities and forget to provide leadership over others' responsibilities. A good leader makes sure delegated tasks are carried out in a timely manner.

Jesus

Jesus was able to keep his priorities straight when facing distractions. While in Capernaum, he was experiencing fruitful ministry. In the synagogue, he taught with astonishing effectiveness and healed a demon-possessed person. On the way home from the synagogue, he went to Peter's mother-in-law and healed her from a fever.

> That evening at sundown they brought to him all who were sick or oppressed by demons. And the whole city was gathered together at the door. And he healed many who were sick with various diseases, and cast out many demons.
>
> ~ Mark 1.32-34

The next morning, Jesus went off to pray and Peter went looking for him. During Jesus' prayer session, the Father must have guided Jesus to move on, despite the successful response in Capernaum, because Jesus told Peter, "Let us go on to the next towns, that I may preach there also, for that is why I came out" (Mark 1.38).

Jesus kept his priorities straight and moved to the next place. Even great success could not distract Jesus from his Heroic Venture.

Leaders can lose focus and fall victim to Tempting Distractions. It is easy to be overwhelmed by the needs. When God gives a vision, project leaders must maintain a disciplined focus on the vision in order to achieve the Heroic Venture.

Questions for Discussion

1. In what ways were Lewis and Clark distracted from their priorities?
2. How did Abraham fall to Tempting Distractions? What about Samson and Jehoash?
3. How have you seen people fall to similar distractions?
4. How did Jesus keep focused on his priorities?
5. How can you recognize a Tempting Distraction? What is the difference between a distraction and an opportunity?

Celebrating Victory

The seventy-two returned with joy, saying, "Lord, even the demons are subject to us in your name!" ~ Luke 10.17

August - September 1806

On August 12, 1806, the day after he was shot in the rear, Lewis met up with Clark's party, which had made it down river without incident. The joy of their reunion was dampened by Lewis' condition. But by August 14 they were back with their friends, the Mandan Indians, who were extremely glad to see the Corps of Discovery alive.

Lewis was disappointed to hear that Pryor's group had not made it to the Mandan village in time to deliver Lewis' letter to Hugh Heney. This hurt the chances of Indian diplomacy, a primary objective of the expedition. Lewis' letter asked Heney to arrange a trip of Sioux chiefs to meet with Jefferson in Washington, D.C. The plan to bring the Sioux into friendly American circles was collapsing. Lewis had the hostile Blackfeet behind him and the dreaded Sioux in front of him.

While the captains were gone, the peace plan they had previously arranged between the Mandans and Arikaras had broken down. Lewis and Clark had made no influence on peace among the plains Indians.

On August 18, they left the Mandan village after compensating Charbonneau and paying compliments to Sacagawea for her outstanding service. She had participated in an amazing transcontinental journey with a newborn baby. The captains said to Charbonneau, "Your woman who accompanied you that long dangerous and fatiguing route to the Pacific Ocean and back deserved a greater reward for her attention and service on the route than we had in our power to give her."

Clark had become so attached to their baby son, Pomp, that Clark offered to adopt him as his own. Years later, Charbonneau sent Pomp to live with Clark to receive an education. After that, Pomp traveled through Europe before becoming a western explorer in his own right.

As the expedition sped down the Missouri, Lewis was recovering from his gunshot wound. They entered Sioux country by the end of August and encountered nine warriors on the bank who signaled for the party to come to shore. Clark assumed they were the Tetons who were so troublesome in 1804.

One of the expedition's canoes was lagging behind, so the captains pulled to shore to let them catch up. As they landed, they heard shots ring out and thought the other canoe was under attack. Lewis hobbled out of his boat and formed the men into a defensive line. Not long afterward, the canoe came safely around the bend.

The Indians were not the hostile Teton, but Yankton Sioux, the friendly tribe they had met in 1804. In fact, one of the Yankton chiefs had traveled to Washington to meet President Jefferson while the expedition was out west. The shot they heard was the Yanktons taking target practice.

With much of the peril behind them, the men were thinking more about home. They were starved for news. A presidential election had taken place but they did not know the outcome. The country could be at war with another country for all they knew. They had become real-life Rip Van Winkles.

They visited Sergeant Floyd's grave at Floyd's Bluff (near modern-day Sioux City, Iowa). On September 6, they encountered a trading vessel and got their first whiskey since July 4, 1805. As each day passed, they were meeting up with more traders, gathering more news. The country was deeply concerned for them, and rumors were plentiful about their status. Some said the Corps of Discovery had been killed, while others said they were captured by the Spanish and working as slaves in their gold and silver mines.

When they were 150 miles from St. Louis, they completely ran out of provisions and trade goods. All they had left were the clothes on their backs, their rifles and ammunition, the cooking kettle, their scientific instruments, and their precious journals. On September 20, the sight of a cow on a hillside triggered spontaneous shouts of joy.

When they reached St. Charles, the village from which they had departed, the men asked permission to fire a salute from the cannon. Their three rounds were answered with three rounds from trading boats on the bank.

The citizens rushed out to greet them, having believed they had long been lost. As celebrations began that would last for many days, Lewis immediately went on to St. Louis to rush his report to President Jefferson.

As Lewis paddled onto the Mississippi, he felt a deep sense of satisfaction at the completion of their epic voyage. He had taken a multi-cultural group of thirty unruly soldiers and guides, molding them into the Corps of Discovery. They had become a tough, hardy, resourceful group of well-disciplined men (and a teenage woman and her baby). Covering eight thousand miles, he brought the entire party back safely, except for one man who died for causes beyond anyone's control.

His passion for the mission never failed him. At the critical moments, he made mostly wise decisions. He had found the most direct route across the continent, just as Jefferson had ordered. He had gathered invaluable scientific data in great detail, adding 178 new plants to the world's scientific knowledge. Against great odds, he returned the specimens and journals safely, including a live prairie dog.

What was previously a blank part of the North American map was now filled in.

This expedition experienced great adventures, tremendous mountains, terrible portages, turbulent rapids, and heartbreaking disappointments. He had conflicts with his men and conflicts with Indians. He faced every kind of physical challenge including extreme cold, mosquitoes, disease, a gunshot wound, and gas-producing roots. He weathered mind-numbing boredom at Clatsop, and terrifying fear at the falls of the Columbia. He had seen a variety of animals, trees, rivers, canyons, cliffs, and Indian tribes that no one man had ever seen. All this was done under the cloud of apparent clinical depression.

As he pulled up to shore in St. Louis, his mind shifted from his Heroic Venture. Now it was time to report to his boss. He shouted to someone on the bank, "when is the next mail leaving St. Louis?"

Lewis' report read:

> In obedience to your orders we have penetrated the Continent of North America to the Pacific Ocean and sufficiently explored the interior of the country to affirm with confidence that we have discovered the most practicable route which does exist across the continent.

Jefferson received the report with pride, saying:

> Of courage undaunted, possessing a firmness and per-severance of purpose which nothing but impossibilities could divert from its direction, careful as a father of those committed to this charge, yet steady in the maintenance of order and discipline, I could have no hesitation in confiding the enterprise to him.

The Heroic Venture had come to successful completion.

◇

EVEN THOUGH some aspects of the Lewis and Clark Expedition were not completely successful, such as the attempt to establish peace among the Indians, there was much to feel satisfied about. It was an amazing accomplishment.

Reporting Back

A significant aspect of a project's completion is reporting to those who are interested in the results, especially leaders over the project. The first thing Lewis did was to report back to Jefferson, the person Lewis was representing, the author of the vision.

In the same way, the Bible talks about leaders who reported back. When Paul returned to Jerusalem after his third missionary journey, he went to see James and the other church leaders. "After greeting them, he related one by one the things that God had done among the Gentiles through his ministry. And when they heard it, they glorified God" (Acts 21.19-20).

After Jesus sent out the seventy-two to preach the Good News to neighboring towns, they returned to excitedly report to Jesus, "Lord, even the demons are subject to us in your name!" (Luke 10.17).

The Blessing of New Friends

The Corps of Discovery developed bonds of friendship they would never forget. In the same way, as Paul went on his missionary journeys, he made disciples among the Gentiles throughout Asia and Europe, fulfilling the mission Jesus gave him. The people he met along the way were not just "projects." They became dearly loved friends. He called the Philippians his "joy and crown" (Phil. 4.1). To the Thessalonians, he said, "For what is our hope or joy or crown of boasting before our Lord Jesus at his coming? Is it not you? For you are our glory and joy" (1 Thess. 2.19-20). The pleasure of the Heroic Venture includes not only the completion of the project, but the blessing of new friends.

What to Expect

In the Heroic Venture many things are uncertain, but some things remain constant. The God who was with Moses, Nehemiah, Paul, and Esther is also with his people today. He still intervenes in the projects of men and women as they experience Committed Team, Internal Complications, Fierce Opposition, Redemptive Setbacks, Personal Suffering, Nagging Discouragement, Prudent Counsel, Tempting Distractions, Dead Vision, and then Renewed Vision.

God Loves Celebration

When a leader has finished strong, faithful to the vision, it is time to celebrate, appreciating those who helped along the way. Paul could say, at the end of his life, "I have fought the good fight, I have finished the race, I have kept the faith" (2 Tim. 4.7).

God instructed Moses to remember the events of the Exodus by celebrating Passover each year:

> This day shall be for you a memorial day, and you shall keep it as a feast to the Lord; throughout your generations, as a statute forever, you shall keep it as a feast. And you shall observe the Feast of Unleavened Bread, for on this very day I brought your hosts out of the land of Egypt.
> ~ Exodus 12.14, 17

Purim

When Haman decided to exterminate the Jews, he cast a lot (called a "pur") to determine the timing of the genocide. The feast of "Purim" is still celebrated today, in remembrance of God's deliverance through Esther. Mordecai sent letters to all the Jews to have them celebrate Purim:

> . . . as the days on which the Jews got relief from their enemies, and as the month that had been turned for them from sorrow into gladness and from mourning into a holiday; that they should make them days of feasting and gladness, days for sending gifts of food to one another and gifts to the poor.
> ~ Esther 9.22

Nehemiah

Nehemiah rebuilt the Jerusalem wall in only fifty-two days, after much opposition. Nehemiah's enemies were "afraid and fell greatly in their own esteem, for they perceived that this work had been accomplished with the help of our God" (Neh. 6.16).

After the project was done, the priests, Levites, gatekeepers, singers and temple servants settled in their towns. Then Nehemiah invited everyone back, organizing a formal celebration that brought the people together in repentance and celebration. Ezra read from the Law of Moses while the people listened attentively, weeping as they heard the Word. The Levites instructed the people about its meaning so they could understand.

Then Nehemiah said the to the assembly:

> "Go your way. Eat the fat and drink sweet wine and send portions to anyone who has nothing ready, for this day is holy to our Lord. And do not be grieved, for the joy of the Lord is your strength."
>
> ~ Nehemiah 8.10

The next day, the people acted on God's Word concerning the Feast of Tabernacles. God had commanded, through Moses, to remember the Jews' Egyptian escape, when they lived in temporary shelters, or tabernacles. So the people brought branches from olive, myrtle, palm, and other shade trees, to build shelters. They joyfully continued the

feast for seven days, as Ezra continued to read the Book of
the Law of God (Neh. 8.13-17).

Hezekiah

King Hezekiah purified the temple after his wicked father,
King Ahaz, had shut the doors years earlier (2 Chron.
28.24-29.19). Hezekiah instructed the Levites to
re-constitute proper worship in the temple by clearing all
unclean items, which took only sixteen days. "Hezekiah
and all the people rejoiced because God had prepared for
the people, for the thing came about suddenly" (2 Chron.
29.36). Hezekiah invited all Israel to a celebration of
Passover in the renovated temple.

When the couriers delivered the king's invitation to the
people, they were met with scorn and ridicule. But when
the time for Passover arrived, a large assembly came to
celebrate with rejoicing and singing. It was going so well
that they decided to extend it seven more days. King
Hezekiah and his officials provided two thousand bulls,
and seventeen thousand sheep and goats for the sacrifice.
There had been nothing like it since the days of Solomon,
250 years before.

When they were done, the people went out to the outlying
towns, smashed the sacred stones, cut down the Asherah
poles, and destroyed the high places and altars throughout
the area.

Joshua

As Joshua was preparing to launch his campaign to conquer the Promised Land, God ordered one of the greatest celebrations of remembrance in the Bible. As the Israelites gathered at the Jordan River, Joshua gave a speech about how God would drive out those inhabiting the land. He instructed the priests to carry the ark into the river, and although it was at flood stage, Joshua said it would cease flowing at the proper time. Just as he promised, as soon as the priests touched the water, the Jordan stood in a heap and stopped flowing, allowing the whole nation to cross near Jericho, at Gilgal.

When they finished crossing, Joshua appointed twelve men, one from each tribe, to stack twelve stones from the middle of the Jordan to be "a sign among you" (Josh. 4.6). These stones were to "be to the people of Israel a memorial forever" (4.7). After many decades of wandering in the desert, they had finally reached the Promised Land!

Solomon

When Solomon finished the construction of the temple, he invited the whole nation to watch the ark being delivered to the Holy of Holies. A huge choir, accompanied by 120 trumpets, cymbals, harps and lyres, joined in praise to the Lord, saying, "For he is good, for his steadfast love endures forever" (2 Chron. 5.13). The temple was filled with a cloud, showing the glory of the Lord.

Solomon pronounced a prayer of dedication to the temple. When he finished, fire came down from heaven and consumed the sacrifices, causing the people to kneel on the pavement, their faces to the ground, giving thanks to the Lord, and worshiping. The king and all the people offered sacrifices totaling twenty-two thousand cattle and twenty-two thousand sheep and goats. The festival went on for fifteen days, and then Solomon "sent the people away to their homes, joyful and glad of heart for the prosperity that the Lord had granted to David and to Solomon and to Israel his people" (2 Chron. 7.10).

Zerubbabel

After many long years of hard work, discouragement, lapses in work, and resumption of work, Zerubbabel finally completed the construction of the temple. Then the people celebrated a dedication with great joy. They offered sacrifices and installed the priests for service, according to the Book of Moses. The next month, they had opportunity to celebrate Passover in the newly constructed temple:

> And they kept the Feast of Unleavened Bread seven days with joy, for the Lord had made them joyful and had turned the heart of the king of Assyria to them, so that he aided them in the work of the house of God, the God of Israel.
>
> ~ Ezra 6.22

The Ultimate Celebration

As leaders face each obstacle, passion keeps them going and wisdom helps them make good choices. Through it all, it is a privilege to represent the Living God, looking forward to that Final Day when the Lord Jesus Christ receives the glory he is due.

The greatest celebration of all is ahead, at the Wedding Banquet of the Lamb:

> After this I looked, and behold, a great multitude that no one could number, from every nation, from all tribes and peoples and languages, standing before the throne and before the Lamb, clothed in white robes, with palm branches in their hands, 10 and crying out with a loud voice, "Salvation belongs to our God who sits on the throne, and to the Lamb!"
>
> ~ Revelation 7.9-10

> Then I heard what seemed to be the voice of a great multitude, like the roar of many waters and like the sound of mighty peals of thunder, crying out, "Hallelujah! For the Lord our God the Almighty reigns. Let us rejoice and exult and give him the glory, for the marriage of the Lamb has come, and his Bride has made herself ready."
>
> ~ Revelation 19.6-7

When he comes, it will be the greatest time of Celebrating Victory in history! Come soon, Lord Jesus.

Questions for Discussion

1. Lewis represented Jefferson's interests in the expedition. How do you represent God's interests in your ministry?
2. Describe how you would feel if you were Lewis and you were coming into St. Charles with your mission completed.
3. How does God show his love of celebration when projects are completed?
4. How did the project leaders of the Bible experience new friendships as they carried out their God-given task? Besides new friendships, what other blessings did they receive due to their obedience?
5. Review the titles of each chapter. Which topics might become the most helpful to you in your Heroic Venture?

Epilogue

GOD HAS been leading people to start new ministries and projects throughout the history of the Bible. Even though God was with the people leading these projects, each one had difficulties along the way. Just like Lewis and Clark's expedition, they faced triumph and heartbreak, but showed courage to the end.

At the outset of their Heroic Venture, God's people had a Compelling Context that led them to a Burning Vision and Personal Calling. As they sought their Vital Preparations, God brought them a Committed Team.

As they carried out their project they faced Internal Complications, Fierce Opposition, Redemptive Setbacks, and Painful Suffering. In response, God's project leaders exemplified Confident Command and made Creative Adjustments.

In spite of good leadership and faithfulness, many experienced Dead Vision, but persevered to find Renewed Vision.

After persevering, Nagging Discouragement often followed them, but they pushed forward, making Daring Decisions and suffering through Patient Waiting. They received Prudent Counsel and fought off Tempting Distractions until they were finally able to experience the joy of Celebrating Victory.

Like others before you, God may be leading you into a vision he wants to bring into reality. He may want to set on fire the spark that flickers within you.

The references that follow are designed to give you concrete, practical tools to help you implement the Heroic Venture God has for your ministry.

References

What Is Wisdom?

God Is a Purposeful God

The God we serve is a God of order and purpose. He has a divine plan to accomplish his holy purpose: the overthrow of the kingdom of darkness through the Lord Jesus Christ. God is moving history in a specific direction, toward the accomplishment of his plan. The purpose of God is the central focus of Scripture, the central focus of history, and the central focus of our personal lives as well. His desire for us is to join him in his plans:

> Go therefore and make disciples of all nations, baptizing them in the name of the Father and of the Son and of the Holy Spirit.
> ~ Matthew 28.19

> But you will receive power when the Holy Spirit has come upon you, and you will be my witnesses in Jerusalem and in all Judea and Samaria, and to the end of the earth.
> ~ Acts 1.8

> And this gospel of the kingdom will be proclaimed throughout the whole world as a testimony to all nations, and then the end will come.
> ~ Matthew 24.14

What a dramatic mission! Preach to all the nations and then the end will come. We must participate in that mission as stewards of his eternal, holy plan. He wants us to be faithful, but more than that, his will is for us to be *fruitful*. "By this my Father is glorified, that you bear much fruit and so prove to be my disciples" (John 15.8).

How to Fulfill God's Purpose

How can the purposes of God be turned into reality? Fulfilling God's purpose requires wisdom. True wisdom is not found in the theoretical classroom, or on an isolated mountain-top, but in the process of *engaging the enemy in battle*. Wisdom is discovered and applied in the midst of the struggle of ministry (Eph. 6.11-18).

Leaders continually face difficult decisions, conflicting information, and unclear implications. There are biblical principles to help leaders make decisions, but sometimes the principles can seem in opposition to each other. For example, we are told to have faith but also to be prudent. Wisdom is needed to apply biblical truth to each situation.

> *Wisdom is choosing what is best*
> *among equally viable truths.*

Wisdom is the understanding that there is danger on either side. You can go too far to the right or too far to the left. You can be open to change when you should stand firm. You can stand firm when you should be open to change.

This is the point of Ecclesiastes. For example:

> For everything there is a season, and a time for every matter under heaven: a time to be born, and a time to die; a time to plant, and a time to pluck up what is planted; a time to kill, and a time to heal; a time to break down, and a time to build up; a time to weep, and a time to laugh; a time to mourn, and a time to dance; a time to cast away stones, and a time to gather stones together; a time to embrace, and a time to refrain from embracing; a time to seek, and a time to lose; a time to keep, and a time to cast away; a time to tear, and a time to sew; a time to keep silence, and a time to speak; a time to love, and a time to hate; a time for war, and a time for peace.
> ~ Ecclesiastes 3.1-8

Wisdom is the ability to choose what is best for the situation. Learning to listen to God, growing in your ability to sense his direction, is the key to wisdom.

> Look carefully then how you walk, not as unwise but as wise, making the best use of the time, because the days are evil. Therefore do not be foolish, but understand what the will of the Lord is.
> ~ Ephesians 5.15-17

> By wisdom a house is built, and by understanding it is established; by knowledge the rooms are filled with all precious and pleasant riches. A wise man is full of strength, and a man of knowledge enhances

his might, for by wise guidance you can wage your war, and in abundance of counselors there is victory.

~ Proverbs 24.3-6

You have an adversary who will attempt to thwart your efforts. To be effective, you must be wise in battle.

Barriers to Using Wisdom

Barriers emerge from within the ranks as well as from without. It is important to be aware of the schemes of the enemy to derail your efforts (2 Cor. 2.11).

◇ *"We've never done it that way before." God has no use for traditions that block his progress.[1] Just because it has always been done a certain way before does not indicate that it remains a wise option.*

◇ *"We're doing fine." Apparent (or real) success can keep you from greater fruitfulness.*

◇ *"Being organized doesn't allow for the leading of the Holy Spirit." God has a plan and is working his plan through his people. You should not be ashamed to follow his example by forming and working a plan.*

◇ *"It doesn't matter what we do—God will bless it.[2] This attitude reflects a lack of discipline. Wisdom suggests consideration of contingencies. Do not confuse trust in God with laziness.*

❖ *"We can do it" rather than "we should do it." Decisions can be based on emotion, available resources, or the easy way out.[3] It is important to keep a clear focus on the vision, engaging in activities which contribute to that vision. There are many good things to invest in, but only a few contribute to the vision. It is poor stewardship to be driven by opportunities rather than by vision. Wisdom demands the effort to consider the implications of decisions, not just taking the easiest option. The path of least resistance often carries a price to pay later.*

❖ *"Fatigue make cowards of us all." Vince Lombardi, legendary coach of the Green Bay Packers, is attributed with this famous line. When you get tired, you are more resistant to new ideas and anything which will tap your already-low resources. What could be an exciting opportunity can instead be seen as overwhelming.*

❖ *"I am afraid I might fail." No one likes to fail, and we have no guarantees that any one project we attempt will turn out the way we plan. Mediocrity is preferable because it is safer. Risky projects bring the prospect of personal failure and humiliation.*

❖ *"I do not like change." It is natural to dread change, but we are commanded to "be transformed by the renewal of your mind" (Rom. 12.2). Flexibility (openness to change) is critical to exercising wisdom.*

❖ *"I might lose my support."[4] Wisdom may dictate action that alienates people or causes controversy among those who financially support the effort. But in the end, if the action is in the best interest of the vision, you must act courageously and sensitively.*

◇ *"We will fight to the bitter end." Armies are known to continue fighting even when they know they will be defeated. Prolonging the war reduces the humiliation of defeat. An attitude of survival can set in. George Barna said, "Encouraging people to pledge themselves to survival is an admission of defeat."[5] Once survival becomes the goal, it is only a matter of time before defeat occurs. Wisdom not only helps achieve victory but also helps minimize losses by recognizing the time to retreat.*

◇ *"My experience tells me this will never work." We can depend on our experience so much that we miss a new thing God wants to do. The story of Peter and Cornelius (see Acts 10) is a classic example. Peter relied on his Jewish experience, which made him resistant to God's desire to save the Gentiles. Watch out for statements like, "I have been here a long time and I know what has been going on. I have been in this ministry for fifteen years and I know this is not going to work." Just because it has not worked before does not mean it will not work this time.*

God Gives Wisdom

Despite the many schemes of the enemy, God promises wisdom when we ask (James 1.5). We can also grow in wisdom by applying ourselves to disciplined effort (Prov.

2.1-6). Learning to make wise choices starts with a healthy fear of the Lord. We are prone to unwise decisions and should have a healthy doubt about our own judgment.

The fear of the Lord is the beginning of wisdom.
~ Proverbs 9.10

Notes

[1] Barna, George. 1992. *The Power of Vision.* Ventura, CA: Regal Books, page 122.

[2] Ibid, page 127.

[3] Ibid, page 146.

[4] Ibid, page 148.

[5] Ibid, page 60.

PREPARE, WORK, REVIEW (PWR):
A Framework for Decision Making, Problem Solving, and Project Leadership

Fan into flame the gift of God. ~ 2 Timothy 1.6

Spontaneous or Pre-Plan?

Some people prefer to pre-plan everything (i.e. being deliberate). Others like to be spontaneous (i.e. being emergent). Sometimes wisdom dictates planning things in advance, while sometimes it is wiser to deal with things as they come. Applying wisdom will mean *choosing what is best among equally viable truths.* So a wise person always keeps the truths of being "deliberate" and "emergent" in mind.[1]

The following simple framework will help you apply wisdom in a variety of situations including decision making, problem solving, personnel issues, and project leadership. This framework is useful for those who tend to be deliberate and those who prefer to be emergent, and is called *PWR: PREPARE, WORK, REVIEW.*

PREPARE (P)
- Pray
- Set the context
- Clarify the values
- Articulate the vision
- Develop alternatives
- Set priorities
- Make assignments

WORK the plan (W)

REVIEW the results (R)
- Evaluate
- Make a new plan

PREPARE (P)

Pray

The most important aspect of wisdom is to seek God. Ask God for wisdom (James 1.5). Cry aloud for wisdom and understanding and seek for it like silver or gold (Prov. 2.1-6). "Keep in step with the Spirit" (Gal. 5.25, NIV) rather than relying on your own wisdom.

Everything starts by seeking God and listening for his guidance.

> *Each aspect of this framework requires a different mindset. Seeking God requires you to **be humble**. "God opposes the proud, but gives grace to the humble" (James 4.6).*

Set the Context

God is a God of history. The New Testament is understood in light of his kingdom purposes, outlined in the Old Testament. The context helps interpret Bible passages. In the same way, good decisions are made in the proper context,[2] like the men of Issachar. They "had understanding of the times, to know what Israel ought to do" (1 Chron. 12.32).

The context provides the compelling background that ignites your passion. It is from the surrounding conditions that you are set into motion. It is not about planning and logic, but gut-level passion.

What is happening in your situation? What led up to this decision, problem, or project? How did you get here? Examine the history leading up to this event to clearly understand the situation. Identify your available resources, including strengths and weaknesses.

Also consider the issues beyond your control, called opportunities and threats. These include information about the community, government, or society at large. For example, if there is heightened awareness of gang violence in your neighborhood, you have an opportunity for starting a gang-prevention ministry.

Clarify the Values

Part of identifying the context is isolating the key values that underlie the activity. Certainly a commitment to

Christ and his word are non-negotiable, but there are other shared values which can be called "expectations" or "assumptions." These "non-negotiables" will affect every activity and decision down the road. It is helpful to go through a process to identify these 3-5 values that will guide your future decision-making.

It is important to clarify expectations so everyone involved is on the same page. A good example is what is known as The Abilene Paradox,[3] which relates to a family who lived near Abilene, Kansas. None of the members of the family wanted to take the hot, dusty, summer drive, without air conditioning, to Abilene, in order to have lunch at a favorite restaurant. But each member thought the other members wanted to go. Since no one said anything, they went, as a group, on that long, unpleasant drive, each person wishing they were somewhere else. Clarifying expectations is essential to the process of "clarifying the values."

> *Be reflective. "Desire without knowledge is not good, and whoever makes haste with his feet misses his way" (Prov. 19.2).*

Articulate the Vision

A key part of applying wisdom is being clear on the task. Noah built an ark. Nehemiah repaired the wall. Esther saved her people from extinction. Moses led his people out of slavery. Joshua led the Israelites into the Promised Land.

Your task might be making a decision about Sunday School curriculum, or planning a deacon meeting.

It is said that those who make great art can envision what the artwork looks like before it is created. Michelangelo is credited with saying he was "releasing" his sculptures from their marble prisons. People of vision can see the completed task in their mind before it happens.

God-given tasks emerge as you submit yourself to him. He gives you burdens, interests, and passions. Pay close attention to those as indicators of God's will (see Reference E, *Discerning God's Will*).

Be Clear

The vision, whatever it might be, needs to be clearly defined so you can challenge people to join you (see Reference D, *How to Implement your Ministry Vision*). Vision stirs people to contribute their talents to achieve the outcome. Effective leaders inspire people by clearly defining the task. Clarity of purpose provides many benefits:

❖ *People can decide if they want to join you in fulfilling the vision or move on to something else. You do not want people on your team who do not support the vision. If they lack commitment to the task, they will cause problems. You are better off with a small number of committed people than a large group with mixed commitment.*

231

⋄ *Clear direction minimizes confusion, giving a sense of confidence and hope. Soldiers die from lack of clarity and direction. If there is confusion about the task, there will be confusion about the details along the way. When there is clarity, everyone knows their assignment. Everyone needs to know how they can contribute to the vision.*

⋄ *Opportunities that contribute to the vision can be anticipated and recognized quickly. Nehemiah was ready when the opportunity arose to explain his vision to the king.*

⋄ *An environment is created where you can say "no" to opportunities that do not contribute to the vision. Wasteful activities and tempting distractions are minimized.*

⋄ *Everyone understands whether progress is being made or not. Clarity makes evaluation easier.*

⋄ *Clarity of purpose helps navigate between vision (faith) and reality (prudence). Keeping the end in mind will help you decide when to be bold and push forward and when to hold back and exercise prudence.*

⋄ *Clear direction inspires people and sets them free to innovate. If you have committed and gifted team members, they will come up with new ideas to achieve the vision. This is the way the body of Christ is designed to work.*

✧ *With a clear understanding of the vision, you can be pro-active, adjusting your actions to fit the need. You can minimize the feeling of being a victim of circumstances[4] by taking control of your own actions in response to the current reality.*

Be Specific

Be specific in the definition of the task. Doing so unleashes tremendous creative energy. In 1961, President John F. Kennedy said, "I believe that this nation should commit itself to achieving this goal, before the decade is out, of landing a man on the moon and returning him safely to earth."[5] This historic challenge stimulated a technological revolution. But it was not the general idea of landing on the moon that carried the power, but the specific language of completing the task by the end of the decade. Nine years later, Kennedy's vision was realized. In the process, hundreds of scientific, medical, and technological breakthroughs were given to the world.

When measurable standards are set, people's behavior changes, because they want to meet the standards. When behavior changes repeatedly over time, habits develop. When habits form in a group of people, a "culture" emerges. Therefore, "Measures shape behavior and behavior creates culture."[6]

Be Passionate

Passion must be the key factor when defining the task. The task emerges from the passion of the leader as he/she is motivated by God's will. The leader ignites passion in others, who then persevere to attain the vision.

> *Be Passionate. "Do not be slothful in zeal, be fervent in spirit, serve the Lord" (Rom. 12.11).*

Prayer, Context, Values, Vision

Once you have defined the task, you have the framework you need to organize around that vision. This makes up the "what." Next you need to determine "how" you are going to accomplish the task. How will you accomplish the vision God has given you?

Develop Alternatives

Once the task is defined, the temptation is to choose the first, most obvious strategy. Instead, you should get counsel from others, or dream about various options that might not have first come to mind. Suspend the tendency to jump to action and take some time to consider the options.

Some activities and decisions are small, so this can be done quickly. Other decisions have serious implications so the process of developing alternatives will take longer.

> *Be imaginative. "Plans are established by counsel; by wise guidance wage war" (Prov. 20.18).*

Set Priorities

Once you have considered some alternative strategies, the next tendency is to try everything. Instead, narrow your options and set priorities consistent with the vision. Evaluate the options in terms of factors like finances, facilities, and personnel.

> Be prudent. "The simple believes everything, but the prudent gives thought to his steps. The prudent sees danger and hides himself, but the simple go on and suffer for it." (Prov. 14.15; 22.3).

Go back and double check your thought process. If you have written something, this is the time to proofread it to make sure it is right. If it is a decision, double-check your process to this point. Did you seek God, set the context, clarify values, articulate the vision, develop alternatives, and set priorities? Are you on the right track?

> Be discerning. "The wisdom of the prudent is to discern his way, but the folly of fools is deceiving." (Prov. 14.8).

Make Assignments
Make a to-do list. Do not leave people guessing about the specifics of their assignment. For each step or role, list a specific person, with a due date. One of the biggest problems in ministry projects is a lack of clarity about assignments. Team members will be frustrated if their job is unclear. Leaders will be frustrated if team members spend time on wasted activities.

In decision making or problem solving, this is the time to choose an option or course of action.

> Be decisive. "All this he made clear to me . . . all the work to be done according to the plan. . . . Be strong and courageous and do it" (1 Chron. 28.19-20).

WORK the Plan (W)

There comes a time to stop talking and planning and take action. This is the time to seek results, not methods. Do not be distracted from implementing the task or decision. During this time to "WORK" the plan, execution is the key. It is far better to execute an average plan than it is to have a great plan that you cannot implement. Winning sports teams are effective in executing their plans. Those who have a great game plan but cannot execute it are the teams who typically lose the game.

Adjust Frequently

Ministry, like warfare, can be described as "an environment of chaotic and rapidly changing conditions." Events seldom go as planned, so frequent adjustment, creativity, and bold innovation are important.

Bobby Bowden, former head football coach at Florida State University said, "You may work all week on a game plan and then get four plays into the game and realize the plan's no good. You have to be able to adjust. You have to build flexibility into your people and strategies."

Creativity is vital in warfare, "It is the leader's creative idea which enables him to lead his men to the most significant victories."[7] Fighter pilot John Boyd taught fellow pilots to engage in the chaos of warfare by continually adjusting and re-adjusting to changing conditions. The model of orientation he uses was called the OODA loop: observation, orientation, decision, action.[8]

Jesus taught the parable of the talents (Matt. 25.14-30) to highlight the steward who was most creative in using his talents to produce a rich return.

Invite Innovation

Team members need a clear enough picture of the task so they can innovate freely. "[Give] the boundaries in which people are free to live out their spiritual gift without asking for permission."[9] Jazz music is an example of innovation within boundaries. Each song has a basic structure in which musicians are free to innovate.

Watch for Extremes

There are two opposite extremes to consider. One is a rigid commitment to the plan despite the changing conditions. The other is a lack of discipline to follow the plan that has been put in place. Some hold on too long; others give up too easily. There is no easy answer. It takes godly wisdom to know when to stay focused and when to go in a different direction.

Be creative. Remember the lessons of the parable of the talents (Matt. 25.14-30).

237

REVIEW the Results (R)

Planning and executing a ministry task is tiring and time consuming. After it is over, the last thing you want to do is evaluate the activity. It is easier to assume that what you did was effective. Time, effort, and resources are wasted when ineffective programs or personnel continue without review.

Evaluation

Successful organizations are ruthless in their evaluation. Fruitfulness in ministry requires relentless evaluation. Since friction occurs (things seldom go according to plan), it is important to review the results and methods in order to make corrections.

The United States military has a commitment to evaluating every mission, believing the most important part of a battle is the debrief. Margaret Wheatley said, "[The Army] has this wonderful process of learning from direct experience called 'After Action Review,' in which everyone involved sits down and discusses three questions: What happened? Why do you think it happened? And what can we learn from it?"[10]

Admiral Jim Stockdale was the highest ranking officer in the Hanoi Hilton, a Vietnamese prison camp. He was greatly admired by his men. Tortured twenty times, he did everything he could to help his fellow prisoners survive. He invented ways to help his men cope with their ordeal, such as an internal communication system that allowed them to deal with the loneliness of confinement. In order to prevent him from being misrepresented on videotape as a "well-treated prisoner," he beat himself with a chair and cut himself with a razor. From this horrific experience, Stockdale developed what is known as "The Stockdale Paradox,"[11] which is:

> *"Retain the faith that you will prevail in the end,*
> *regardless of the difficulties,*
> *AND AT THE SAME TIME,*
> *confront the most brutal facts of your current reality,*
> *whatever they might be."*

Stockdale understood that great leaders are merciless in their evaluation.

In sports, the best teams are those who make good "half-time adjustments." They evaluate what happened and make adjustments to their game plan while they have time to reflect and chart a new course.

Celebrate

Another essential element of "REVIEW" is celebrating what God has done. As you pray with great fervor for his blessing, be intentional to thank him along the way for his answers. Also appreciate people who contributed to the vision.

Ed Delahanty has the fourth greatest batting average in major league baseball history, but he failed 65.4% of the time. Celebrate the .346 batting average, not the 65.4% failure rate.

Even when the results are disappointing, the team's energy has not been wasted. The team has prayerfully prepared, working with trust in God. You cannot always see the whole picture of what God had in mind for your project.

Learn

The evaluation is a good time to remind the team that setbacks are inevitable and redeemable if there is a willingness to learn from them. The most devastating defeats can be fertile ground for improvement. Jack Welch, former CEO of General Electric, said this about the lessons of the 2005 Hurricane Katrina crisis:

> Immunity to crises comes from learning. Crises teach us where the system is broken and how to repair it so it won't break again. Ultimately, learning is why disasters, in business and in nature, have the potential to make the organizations that survive them so much stronger in the long run.[12]

The main reason to REVIEW is to make adjustments. Learning and adjusting are the keys to wise leadership. After REVIEW, re-visit the other parts of PWR. Go back and PREPARE (pray, re-set the context, confirm or modify the values and task, develop new alternatives and priorities, check the facts, and give new individual assignments). WORK your new plan. REVIEW the results. This cycle will help you learn.

Pray	WHAT?	Humble
Set the context		Reflective
Articulate the vision		Passionate
Develop alternatives	HOW?	Imaginative
Set priorities		Prudent
Check the facts		Discerning
Make assignments		Decisive
WORK the plan		Creative
REVIEW the results		Reflective

REVIEW is the most neglected part of PWR, but also the most critical. It is the evaluation which brings improvement for the next task. Nehemiah needed to evaluate because of Sanballat. Peter faced the surprise of Cornelius. Gideon had to adjust his plan when God told him to reduce the size of his troops. Paul had to change direction after the Macedonian vision. You must be open to the Holy Spirit and not be rigid or dogmatic.

Be reflective again. "Poverty and disgrace come to him who ignores instruction, but whoever heeds reproof is honored. Whoever ignores instruction despises himself, but he who listens to reproof gains intelligence" (Prov. 13.18; 15.32).

PWR Example

To show how PWR is applicable to even the most basic activities of life, consider this example: A three-year-old boy is playing with blocks and asks his father to play with him.

Pray. The father has many alternatives for his time but quickly prays and decides it is best to give his son some attention.

Context. The father quickly goes through a mental process: playing with blocks is good for kids' motor skills. Fathers and sons playing together is good for bonding. His little boy loves to build with toys and has some ideas about how to play with them. The father knows a variety of ways that blocks can be used for fun, since he remembers playing with blocks himself.

Vision. In a short conversation, they agree that the primary vision is to build a tower in order to knock it down in spectacular fashion.

Alternatives. They discuss various ways to build the tower before its demise. They can build for speed, they can build to a certain height, they can build it with all the same colors or with some visually attractive design.

Priorities. After a short discussion, they agree that building for speed up to a height equal to the son's height is the preferable alternative.

Fact check. They quickly review what they are doing: building to a certain height in order to knock it down, making sure there are enough blocks to build it to the desired height. They will have to re-design to build to a lesser height if they do not have enough blocks for the original plan.

Assignments. They divide up duties. Dad is assigned to separate the blocks by size. The son will build the tower with Dad's frequent consultation. They are both satisfied with the arrangement and clear on their roles.

WORK the plan. They begin building, adjusting as they go, in order to make sure it does not fall over before it reaches its desired height. At the end, the son gets the honor of kicking the tower over with a great crash.

REVIEW the results. They decide to do it again, but this time with a different building design that will make it go higher. They build, and destroy, with great satisfaction and lasting memories.

This is a silly and simplistic example, but one that shows all the essential steps of applying wisdom to a task. Most ministry activities are much more complex and require greater effort. But the same mental process is used.

At each step along the way, errors can be made that will sabotage the success of the endeavor. For example, if the discussion of context is skipped over, there can be an argument between father and son over their differing hopes. If the vision is not defined clearly, another conflict can ensue. If alternatives are not considered and then priorities set, there could be multiple failed attempts before the satisfactory experience occurs, and by that time the father or son might have given up in frustration, making it less than a happy family moment. If individual assignments are not made there could be hurt feelings ("But I wanted to kick the tower over, not you, Daddy"), making future activities less likely.

Summary

You can apply PWR as you fan into flame your spiritual gift (2 Tim. 1.6). Victory is found when there is wise preparation, creatively executed under the guidance of the Holy Spirit, with rigorous review.[13]

Dwight Eisenhower, leader of the Allied Forces in World War II, said, "In preparing for battle, I have always found that plans are useless, but planning is indispensable."[14] Eisenhower knew that the process of preparation was more important than the actual plan itself. Plans can be thrown out, but the process of thinking and discussing is critical.

The PWR framework is helpful to many areas of personal or ministry life, such as overseeing a ministry task, planning a day of your life, leading your family, or making a decision.

Notes

[1] Mintzberg, Henry. 1994. *The Rise and Fall of Strategic Planning.* New York, NY: The Free Press, page 24.

[2] Barna, George. *The Power of Vision*, page 85.

[3] Goodstein, Leonard, Nolan, Timothy, Pfeiffer, J. William. 1993. *Applied Strategic Planning.* New York, NY: McGraw-Hill, page 152.

[4] Barna, George. *The Power of Vision*, page 110.

[5] Kennedy, John F. May 25, 1961, Special Message to the Congress on Urgent National Needs.

[6] Labovitz, George, and Rosansky, Victor. 1997. *The Power of Alignment: How Great Companies Stay Centered and Accomplish Extraordinary Things.* New York, NY: John Wiley & Sons, Inc., page 156.

[7] Mrazek, James. 1968. *The Art of Winning Wars.* New York, NY: Walker Books.

[8] Hammonds, Keith H. June 2002. *The Strategy of the Fighter Pilot.* Fast Company, pages 100-115.

[9] This quote is from a March-April 1999 NetFax interview with Bill Easum at http://www.ntcumc.org/ArcMyC/MyC9903.html. The idea is fully developed in Bill Easum's book, *Growing Spiritual Redwoods*, 1997. Nashville, TN: Abingdon.

[10] Insight and Outlook. November 1996. *The New Science of Leadership: An interview with Margaret Wheatley.* http://www.scott london.com/insight/scripts/wheatley.html.

[11] Collins, Jim. 2001. *Good to Great.* New York, NY: HarperCollins Publishers, page 86.

[12] Welch, Jack. September 2005. *The Five Stages of Crisis Management.* Opinion Journal. www.opinion.journal.com/editorial/feature.html?id=110007256.

[13] In other contexts I have referred PWR as "SET ON FIRE." *PWR* is a simplified version of *SET ON FIRE*:
S - Seek God
E- Environment identified
T - Task defined
O - Options set
N - Narrowed priorities
F - Fact check
I - Individual assignments
R - Run
E - Evaluate
The key to PWR or SET ON FIRE is the constant cycle of learning and adjusting to changing conditions.

[14] Charlton, James, ed. 2002. *The Military Quotation Book*. New York: St. Martin's Press, page 5.

Projects:
The Outlet for Ministry Passion

Passion and vision must find an outlet. They beg for a vehicle.
Projects are that vehicle.

THE DEFINITION of a project is "an effort with a beginning and an end that must be completed within defined constraints of time, resources, or quality."

There are many examples of projects in the Bible (see Reference H). Likewise, there are many projects that take place in the life of the church. Every time you conduct a service of any kind, including the Sunday morning service, it is a project. Any time you design a new program, it is a project. When you have a meeting, such as an elder meeting, a meeting of Sunday School teachers, a counseling session, or a staff meeting, it is a project. Events, like an outreach event or a retreat, are all projects.

Projects are one-time events, not ongoing tasks or responsibilities. But even ongoing responsibilities might involve projects along the way.

Projects are completed within defined constraints of either time, resources, or quality.

Time

There may be due dates or deadlines involved. The project may have to be completed by a certain date, or the event may need to be completed in a certain time frame. For example, the launching of a new program for evangelism may need to begin within the next twelve months because the leader is moving to another city in the next year.

Resources

There may be limits to how much money can be spent or how much time people can give to the project. The church may want to have a retreat in Hawaii, but that may be outside the budget. There may be constraints on the availability of equipment. The community center you want to use may be booked the day you want to celebrate a church event.

Quality

There needs to be an understanding of the expected level of quality for the project. When God gave Moses the specifications of the tabernacle, he gave great detail about what kind of materials he wanted to use, and how he wanted it constructed. On another occasion, God whittled Gideon's ten thousand-member army down to three hundred men in order to show his greatness. Some projects demand extravagance, while others can be done with very few resources.

Example

There is a classic example of project constraints in Ron Howard's 1995 movie, *Apollo 13*. The three astronauts suffered a critical equipment malfunction in space, preventing their moon landing, and threatening their safe return to earth. The crew's air supply needed to be re-designed or they would die of carbon dioxide poisoning.

Six engineers walked into a room with boxes of miscellaneous items that would be available on the spacecraft. They were given the job of inventing a square filter box that would fit into a round receptacle. Dumping the contents on the table, the leader said to the group, "We have to come through. We got to find a way a way to make this [square box] fit into the hole for this [round cylinder] using nothing but that [pointing to the junk on the table]."[1]

They had a specific task that was constrained by time, quality, and available resources. If they took too long the men would die. Only what was available on the spacecraft could be used to build this device. Their design had to fit a specific, precise standard.

They designed the filter using pages of their flight manual and duct tape, but it worked, and the astronauts made it home safely.

Key Principles of Successful Projects

Preparation is key to the success of any project. The more complex the project, the more time you have to spend in preparation. The following steps imply a complicated project. Less complicated tasks will require less preparation.

The steps to follow in any project can be found in the acronym "PWR" (see Reference B).

P   PREPARE
W   WORK
R   REVIEW

1. First, seek God to guide you on the project.

2. Identify the context by asking these questions:

    a. How did this come about? What were the compelling factors that led to this idea? What things were happening in the community, in my own life, or the lives around me that brought me to this project?

    b. Who is involved? Who will benefit? Who will serve? Who helped me come to this point?

    c. Why am I doing this? Why now?

    d. What are the underlying values, assumptions, or convictions?

    e. What resources (people, money, things) are available?

f. What are the strengths, weaknesses, opportunities, and threats?

3. Describe the purpose of this task. In specific terms, what results are desired at the end? In many projects, you might have a number of sub-purposes (objectives), but there should be one primary purpose to every project, even though you might be accomplishing a number of things at once. For example, when you host a training event on evangelism, the primary purpose might be "to equip the saints for service." But you might have other objectives such as "networking with other churches," or "developing leadership in the church."

Or, your primary purpose may be to "develop a potential leader," and the training and fellowship issues are secondary objectives. In either case, you must identify a primary purpose. Having a clear, primary purpose will help you make decisions later when you run into difficult decisions. Knowing the primary purpose helps you keep your priorities straight and lead your people properly.

A vision statement describes the strategic intent of the activity. It tells someone what the end product looks like. In 1-3 sentences, the vision statement should include:

❖ *What do you want to accomplish?*

◇ *Who are you targeting (ethnicity, geographic, economic, personality, age, gender, need)?*

◇ *What are the constraints or boundaries (time, resources, or other)?*

◇ *How is this distinctive from other similar efforts?*

An example of a vision statement for a church plant would be:

> Over the next four years, we will plant a church that is led by someone from the community, in the Ironbound neighborhood of Newark. We will focus on the Portuguese population with an emphasis on establishing ministry to children that creates relationships with their parents.

Notice that the statement meets all the criteria. It answers the "Who, What, When, How" questions, and is distinctive.

A poor example of a vision statement would be:

> We will be faithful to God by sharing the Gospel. As people accept Christ, we will disciple them and form a church.

Notice that this statement fails all the criteria. It does not mention a target audience. It does not mention any time, resource, or quality constraint, so it is not a true project. It is passive in its language about what is to be accomplished. Finally, it provides little to distinguish the activity from others who might be doing the same thing.

Vision statements need to inspire people to join you. The above example does little to inspire people to attempt great things for God.

4. Break the task down into 3-5 major pieces. All projects, even complex ones, can be broken down into major components.

    For example, when a company plans to make an airplane, they divide the plane into its major components: the wing, the fuselage, the tail, etc. Then they build each component separately and put them all together. In a project as complicated as the Summer Olympic Games, organizers can break the event down into major categories as well. For example, they might organize around a) competitions, b) housing for athletes and officials, c) interface with local government authorities, d) transportation, and e) security.

    In a worship service, you might break up the project into:

    a. sermon preparation

    b. equipment and technical support

    c. greeting/hosting

    d. music

    e. announcements

5. Brainstorm options in the various areas that need to be covered. Brainstorming is the process of quick-paced discussion about ideas, without evaluating the ideas. People are encouraged to join in, providing even the most outrageous ideas, in order to get creativity flowing.

Brainstorming is effective because it presents the maximum number of ideas in a short period of time and it allows the participants to spark each others' creativity. The brainstorming process should include as many people as possible who have knowledge of the subject. Encourage everyone to participate because people will be loyal to the vision if they are involved in the process from the beginning.

When leading brainstorming sessions[2], you should:

    a. Be clear about what's being discussed so you do not have too many topics at once. For example, if you are talking about location for a retreat, do not confuse the session by also brainstorming about the food for the retreat. If unrelated ideas are raised, make sure to write them down for discussion at a later time.

b. Make sure it is a safe, relaxed, and playful environment where no one's ideas will be criticized. (Food always helps to create a relaxed setting).

c. Assign someone to make the ideas visible, using a whiteboard or easel. Number the ideas as you write them down so you can reference them.

d. Have a warm-up exercise to help people start thinking in the right direction. For example, if you are going to brainstorm about designing a new member's class, spend ten minutes presenting ideas about membership classes from other churches. Or share part of an article on the importance of membership. Encourage participants to start thinking in the direction of your discussion.

e. Try to build momentum and excitement. Encourage people to keep adding ideas, even if you think you have enough ideas. That next idea could be the best one.

If you are working on the project by yourself and cannot get help from others, take the time to brainstorm by yourself. Do not act on your first ideas. Try to develop some creative alternatives.

6. Begin bringing order to the chaos of ideas by narrowing the options through prioritizing, combining, eliminating, or modifying the ideas. This can be done

during or after the meeting, as a group or individually. For longer projects:

    a. Narrow your time frame to no longer than twelve months. Most situations change too much to set goals and plans beyond one year.

    b. Create a "not now" list for good ideas whose time has not yet come. Review the list later.

7. Further narrow ideas by forming some planning assumptions or constraints.

    a. Identify how much money is available, or how much money will be needed to complete this project. Include other resources that may be needed.

    b. Consider how your ideas are affected by facilities. Are facilities available? Are they the proper size? Do they meet your needs?

    c. Make a guess about attendance or other assumptions that will drive the scope of the project.

8. Finish narrowing by listing specific action steps. The more complex the project, the more important it becomes to have the plan in writing (see Tables 1 and 2 as examples).

a. List all tasks to be completed. To do this, you will need to mentally picture the whole event from start to finish, imagining in your mind's eye all that will need to take place. If you do not do this, you will miss key details.

b. Group the tasks logically. For example, if you have a number of items that require shopping at the store, combine them into one shopping task, if possible.

c. For each task, consider if another task has to be completed first. For example, one of the tasks for a social might be "choosing a theme." Since "buying the decorations" cannot be done until someone has chosen the theme, "choosing the theme" is called a "predecessor."

d. Establish deadlines to keep the project on schedule.

e. Put the tasks in a logical time sequence, with the first deadline listed first.

9. Fact-check the action steps. Make sure you have thought through everything. You should go through a second round of imagining the event or project in your mind. Consider the following:

a. People

b. Money

c. Equipment and technology

d. Information

e. Facilities

f. Prayer support

g. Proper approval

h. Communication

i. Materials and supplies

j. Time for final review

k. Are there unnecessary tasks? Does anything overlap?

l. Are there unnecessary predecessors?

m. Are the tasks realistic?

n. Are the tasks measurable? Are they clear enough to minimize confusion?

o. Do people have the tools they need to do the job?

p. Are the tasks consistent with the relative level of quality desired or availability of resources (e.g. is the van available that weekend?)

q. Have you considered the cost of alternatives?

r. Can you meet the constraints for money, quality, or time?

10. Delegate individual assignments.

a. Make sure you know the project's purpose, and have communicated it to others.

b. Communicate the expectations of quality, resources, and time.

c. Tell each team member how often you want reports on their progress.

d. Make sure people know what is assigned to them. Do not assume they will know.

11. Run the project by working the plan.

a. Monitor the written task list daily or weekly (depending on project phase). When projects get near to completion, you will have to refer to your task list more often.

b. Follow up on delegated tasks. Some people will need more checking than others. Some will appreciate you checking on them as a show of support and others will be irritated, thinking you do not trust them. Be wise in leading each person.

c. Look for changes in assumptions or events. Make adjustments accordingly.

d. Make vendors bid competitively. If you can get three bids on items, you almost always get close to the best price. Even if you have a relationship with someone, or have always done business with them in the past, it is still worth the effort to shop. You will often find a better price.

e. Run effective meetings. Come prepared with an agenda. Set the time and location for the next meeting while you are together. Clarify what everyone's next steps are.

f. Keep notes on successes, failures, and ideas. If you do a similar project later, you will appreciate having the notes to help you make adjustments. Do not assume you will remember. Research shows that repeated events go 20% easier if you learn from your past experience.[3] Keep notes to remind yourself what to do (or not do) next time.[4]

12. Evaluate the project.

    a. Get feedback from the participants.

    b. Have a formal review of the event. Even though you think you know everything about the successes of the event, you should still collect information from those who were involved. Keep the results and review them again for next time. Compare results against your stated purpose. Did you get the results you hoped to get? Ask these questions:

        1) What went well?

        2) What did not go well?

        3) What should we change, add, or delete?

        4) What should we retain or increase?

    c. Celebrate victory at the conclusion of the project. Despite what the results were, and despite how satisfied or dissatisfied you were, thank God for his provision. Thank those who contributed to the project.

    d. Report back to whomever needs to hear about the results.

    e. Take any corrective action revealed in your evaluation.

Project Killers

There are a number of common mistakes that project leaders make that can hinder a project.

1. Over-commitment to quality.

    You can spend too much time and money trying to get it "just right" and miss the goal of excellence within reason. Hold to a high standard, but be careful not to kill the project by unreasonable expectations. The most common problems are:

    a. Overspending money. Many failed projects run out of money before they are finished. Make sure you have adequate resources, or are able to make adjustments if money does not come in as expected.

    b. Taking too much time. Projects often have a time constraint. Pay attention to deadlines.

2. Problems with expectations.

    a. Unclear expectations. If people are confused about their assignments, the project can fail. Be clear, and follow up to ensure clarity.

    b. Disagreement about expectations. Some people will know exactly what you want, but will undermine you because they have their own agenda. If you discover this, you need to correct them, reassign them, or ask them to leave the project. Do not let others sabotage the project.

3. Too many meetings. Have meetings only when they are necessary. Think twice before calling a meeting. Can it be handled over the phone, one-on-one, or in writing? If you have a meeting, be prepared with an agenda so you make good use of the time and effort.

4. Poor leadership. Most projects fail because of poor leadership. Seek to grow in all areas of leadership. Learn from your mistakes.

Project Example: Women's Retreat

The following is a step-by-step example of following the *PWR* framework for hosting a women's retreat.

1. You seek the Lord's guidance, then you identify the environment. You have just conducted a weekend door-to-door evangelism event and thirty-two women expressed a commitment to Christ. Now you need a way to take a next step with these new believers.

2. You define the purpose. You decide that getting the thirty-two women oriented into the life of the church is the primary purpose. You want to see all thirty-two women start coming to church and become involved in a weekly Bible study.

3. You break the retreat into major pieces. You decide on these areas:

    a. Transportation

    b. Speaker/teaching

    c. Activities

    d. Food

    e. Follow-up

5. Then you begin brainstorming options regarding the retreat. What kind of program should we have? Where should it be? How will we follow up? What do we need to do that maximizes the probability the new believers will come to weekly church activities after this is over?

6. After that, you prioritize your brainstorming ideas. You eliminate some ideas or combine others in order to get a picture of the details.

7. You develop planning assumptions. You decide that out of the thirty-two women you invited, twenty of them will attend. You guess that fifteen women, who are already members of the church, will join them, for a total attendance of thirty-five. You find that you have been given $1000 for the retreat and have to work within those figures. This will help you make further decisions.

8. You make a list of tasks that have to be completed (see Table 1). You think through the whole retreat from start to finish, imagining what will take place, so that you do not forget any important details. You decide to delegate some of this thinking to other people who are doing some of the work. You ask them to report back to you in a week about their areas of responsibility.

9. You do a sanity check to see if you have covered all your bases. You find that you forgot to include the development of a detailed budget. So you add that to your list of items.

10. You communicate assignments to people on the retreat team. You make sure they know their duties, how much money they have to work with, and when they are to report back to you. You answer their questions and make sure they know how to begin taking their first steps.

11. You set the time for the next meeting and clarify what your next steps are going to be.

12. You work your task list, monitoring it periodically to see how progress is being made.

13. You check back with people who have been given assignments, encouraging them and making sure they have the information or tools they need to get the job done.

14. You are on the lookout for unexpected events. You are not troubled or surprised when they occur, but react to them creatively and joyfully, knowing God is with you. You seek the help of others on your team to come up with ideas on how to adjust to changes.

15. You are keeping notes on lessons learned so you can remember them later.

16. A few days before the event, you double check to see if everything is done. People may have forgotten what they were supposed to do, so you remind some of them about their tasks.

17. When the time for the retreat comes, you have created a new task list with all the things that have to occur at the event. You monitor it closely throughout the day, improvising as needed.

18. You collect feedback from the ladies who attended the retreat, and also from the team who worked with you to host the retreat.

19. You write up your own notes on what happened and what you learned from the event. For example, you write down that fourteen new women came to the retreat, in addition to seventeen existing members. You note that there was not enough food for dinner one night.

20. Two weeks after the retreat, you find out that three of the women from the initial outreach are coming to the weekly ladies Bible study. You think about the retreat and ask some questions:

    a. What did we do well that helped us get the three women into a weekly Bible study?

    b. What could we have done better to generate more interest so that more women would have become a part of the life of the church?

21. You thank all the people on the team who contributed to the retreat. You find ways to celebrate what God has done. In this case, you host a tea for the ladies who served on the retreat team, thank them each publicly, and chat about the results.

22. You create a file containing your plans, notes, and a review of the results where you (or someone else) can refer to your ideas when conducting a similar event in the future.

Table 1 - Example Task List

First Baptist Women's Retreat, May 15-17, 2043
Purpose: Draw new believers into the church through retreat
Planning Assumptions: Budget $1000, 35 in attendance

#	Task	Responsible	End	Pred.	Cost
1	Form committees	Committee	4/8		$400
2	Select location	Committee	4/1		
3	Theme	Committee	4/1		
4	Set dates	Committee	4/1		
5	Announce on Sunday	Kerry	4/9		
6	Book location	Marilyn	4/8		
7	Coordinate transportation	Desha	4/29	1, 2, 4	
8	Plan worship	Carla	4/15		
9	Assemble worship team	Carla	4/15		
10	Rehearse worship	Carla	4/29	9	
11	Assemble prayer team	Tanya	4/15		
12	Select/contact teacher	Rosalyn	4/15	3	
13	Get outline from teacher	Rosalyn	4/29	12	
14	Create schedule	Committee	4/8		
15	Create invitations and flyers	Jenny	4/15	8,12	$10
16	Final announcement at church	Kerry	4/16		
17	Mail invitations	Anna	4/19		$20
18	Create program	Janice	5/6		$25
19	Register attendees	Harriet	5/6		
20	Plan social activities	Anna	4/22		
21	Send prayer needs to prayer team	Committee	5/6	11	
22	Plan group prayer w/ leaders	Tanya	4/22		
23	Review/debrief retreat	Committee	6/8		

Table 2 - Project Chart Example

Project Title	**Evangelistic Outreach, 6/15/02** *Version: 1 Date: 3/15/02*	
Project Definition:	Host an evangelistic outreach in Oaklawn - to make our presence known in the community, to win people to Christ, and draw them into our Oaklawn Fellowship Church	
Project Completion Date:	June 15, 2002	
Project Leader:	Angie	
Project Team Members:	Daren, Matt, Lyn, Audrey	
Suggested Phases and/or Steps:		**Date Due**
Preparation		
1. Meet to discuss event, place, date, budget, activities, sound, speaker, MC, musicians, PR and follow-up, *Team*		3/15/02
2. Send invitation/request to musicians/speaker/volunteers, *DB*		3/19/02
3. Request use of community center, and UAC chairs/tables, DB		3/20/02
4. Plan activities; get supplies & prizes for each activity, *AP/MP*		3/22/02
5. Draft program/schedule; create/copy/distribute flyers, *LC*		4/1/02
6. Plan food, setup/cleanup (kind, qantity, paper goods), *AH/AP*		4/26/02
7. Make response cards (for those wanting more info, give their lives to Christ, etc.), *LC/AH*		5/10/02
8. Hold project team meeting to update and clarify, *Team*		5/29/02
Implementation		
9. Contact speaker/musicians with final details, *DB*		5/30/02
10. Distribute flyers to community, *Team*		6/1 &6/8
11. Purchase food and supplies, *AH*		6/10/02
12. Write thank you for speaker/musicians & bring to event, *LC*		6/12/02
13. Get tables/chairs from church & set up at location, *DB/MP*		6/15/02
14. Bring sound equipment, set up and run equipment, *AP/AH*		6/15/02
15. Bring grill and supplies and grill food, *MP/LC*		6/15/02
16. Meet speaker (*DB*), musicians (*AP/MP*), volunteers (*AH/LC*)		6/15/02
17. Collect all response cards and give to Daren, *Team*		6/15/02
Wrap-Up		
18. Break down/return sound equip/tables/chairs & clean, *DB/MP*		6/15/02
19. Follow up people who made decisions, want more info, *Team*		6/16-6/19
20. Meet as project team and evaluate all aspects of event, *Team*		6/20/02
Project Milestone Dates:	1. Preparation Phase Completion	5/29/02
	2. Implementation Phase Completion	6/15/02
	3. Wrap-Up Phase Completion	6/20/02
Project Resources Needed:	1. Budget for food (for how many people?) and activities (what and how much?), honorariums for speaker and musicians (how much)? 2. Cost of creating & reproducing flyers and rental of community center	
Comments, Questions, Concerns:	1. Are we targeting all of Oaklawn? Should we advertise in the paper? 2. Do we want to have anyone from the community give a testimony of how they met Christ during this event? 3. What will we do if it rains on the 15th?	

◇

Notes

[1] Howard, Ron. 1995. *Apollo 13*. http://www.scottlondon.com/insight/scripts/wheatley.html. Burbank, CA: MCA Universal Pictures.

[2] Fast Company. March 2001. *Seven Secrets of Good Brainstorming* at www.fastcompany.com/change/change_feature/kelley.html.

[3] Salvendy, Gavriel, editor. 1982. *Handbook of Industrial Engineering*. New York, NY: John Wiley and Sons, Inc, page 4.3.10.

[4] Baker, Sunny and Kim. 1998. *The Complete Idiot's Guide to Project Management*. New York, NY: Macmillan Publishing, page 209.

How to Implement Your Ministry Vision

Y<small>OU HAVE</small> a passion for a new ministry. You believe it is from God. Now what do you do? How can you bring it from vision to reality?

First, realize that if your vision is of God, he will bring it about. Trust him to do the work and to guide you despite your weaknesses or past failures. Learn from the people God has used in Scripture. "For whatever was written in former days was written for our instruction, that through endurance and through the encouragement of the Scriptures we might have hope" (Rom. 15.4).

Second, your passion will help you push through the obstacles that emerge along the way. If you add wisdom to your passion, you will strengthen your cause. But no amount of wisdom can overcome a lack of passion.

Third, some visions will be larger than others. Some are simple, one-time events. Others are large, lifelong, and ambitious projects. The larger and more complex the vision, the more preparation and planning needed, so as you consider the following guidelines, remember to apply them according to the level of complexity of your vision.

There are some key principles you should consider as you seek to implement your vision.

⬦ *Be able to communicate the vision to others.*

⬦ *Gather people around you to help you carry it out.*

⬦ *Take leadership of the vision and continuously apply energy to it.*

⬦ *Be willing to start small and let it grow.*

Communicate the Vision

The task needs to be clear enough to invite others to join you.[1] Very rarely will you be involved with any ministry task where you will not have to clearly communicate the vision.

When businesses consider a new project they often refer to the "4 P's: Product, Price, Place, and Promotion."[2] The "4 P's" are an effective tool you can use to communicate and implement your vision.

Product

What is the product that you want to produce? Is it a youth ministry? A men's retreat? A new church? A drug recovery ministry? Clearly outline the purpose of the product or ministry and what result you are trying to achieve. You can do this by answering some basic questions.

1. Whom do you serve? Think through the characteristics of the people your ministry will serve. Be specific about age, gender, ethnicity or other characteristics of your target group.

2. What is the primary strength of this ministry?

3. What is the primary way to measure the success of this ministry?

4. What significant "next steps" can be taken to move the ministry forward?

Price

How will the finances work in this ministry? How much will it cost? Think through all areas of resources including the people you need, facilities, equipment, and other things that are listed specifically in Reference C (see "Fact Check").

Place

How will you deliver your service to the people you want to serve? In business terms, this is the "distribution" question. Will you have people come to your location? Will you take it to them? Is there something that you will physically give them or is it a service?

Promotion

How will you get the word out to those you want to serve? How will you connect the product with your target group?

Gather People Around You

You will need help to carry out your vison. At minimum, you will certainly need prayer support. But you also might need financial support or professional advice. You might need people to fill other roles, working under your leadership.

You need people to join you with strengths you do not have. You probably cannot pull off your vision without help from others with different expertise and perspective.

Once you have developed answers to your "4 P's" you can begin sharing the vision with others and see who God brings to your team.

In some cases, you should consider working under the leadership of an existing church or organization. It is good to have spiritual covering to protect you and give you leadership. Churches and ministries often have an existing network of resources from which you can draw. Starting your own ministry is very difficult and can be overwhelming. Learning from others and enjoying their fellowship can be an encouraging experience.

Take Leadership

Once you see others joining you, it is important to provide persistent energy to the task. People around you will get discouraged. Others will drop out. You need to continue articulating the vision and providing clear leadership. You do this by continuing to ask the four questions:

1. Whom do you serve?

2. What is the primary strength of this ministry?

3. What is the primary way to measure the success of this ministry?

4. What significant "next steps" can be taken to keep moving the ministry forward?

At every step of your journey, you will need to review these questions and adjust to changing conditions.

Start Small

Pilot-testing is an excellent way to start projects. Start with something small and see how it works. Ask for feedback. If it is fruitful, try something bigger.

For example, rather than begin a prison ministry, try visiting a prison a few times and see if your visits are productive. Then expand to something more formal.

Think about Jesus' principle of the mustard seed. The Kingdom starts small and unseen. But it grows into something that can be seen and enjoyed by all. Start your vision on a small scale and be patient. God can grow it over time. God is able to set it on fire. Visions that are of God will be attractive, and people will join where they see God at work.

Notes

[1] Buckingham, Marcus. 2005. *The One Thing You Need to Know*. New York, NY: Free Press, page 197.

[2] McCarthy, E. Jerome. 1981. *Basic Marketing: A Managerial Approach*. 7th ed. Homewood, IL: Richard D. Irwin.

Discerning God's Will

HOW CAN you know if your vision is of God or just your own idea?

Understand the Big Picture

In order to discern God's will, you need a firm understanding of his purposes in the world. If you start from your own perspective, you start from a reference point that is too small to give guidance. You will become confused, overestimate your importance, and lose your way. You have to start with *what is important to God* and how you fit into his grand design.

Navigators never use their own location as a reference point, but use fixed points like the North Pole, the sun, or the North Star. In the same way, you should never start with your own experience to discern God's will. Instead use God's unchanging plan, revealed in his Word, as your fixed reference point.

The Kingdom of God was Jesus' chief concern.[1] He instructed us to "seek first his Kingdom" (Matt. 6.33).

The Kingdom is the story of Jesus':

⋄ **Conquest over his enemy.** *Then comes the end, when he delivers the kingdom to God the Father after destroying every rule and every authority and power. For he must reign until he has put all his enemies under his feet (1 Cor. 15.24-25).*

⋄ **Rescue of people from the kingdom of darkness.** *He has delivered us from the domain of darkness and transferred us to the kingdom of his beloved Son (Col. 1.13).*

⋄ **Coronation where he reigns forever.** *The kingdom of the world has become the kingdom of our Lord and of his Christ, and he shall reign forever and ever (Rev. 11.15.)*

Our lives need to be oriented around his kingdom purposes.

Be a Living Sacrifice

When you understand the Big Picture, you recognize your role is to represent Christ in the world, being "conformed to the image of his Son" (Rom. 8.29). When you surrender yourself to the work of representing Christ and his Kingdom, no matter the cost, you are in a place to begin understanding his will. Romans 12.1-2 says:

> I appeal to you therefore, brothers, by the mercies of God, to present your bodies as a living sacrifice,

holy and acceptable to God, which is your spiritual worship. Do not be conformed to this world, but be transformed by the renewal of your mind, that by testing you may discern what is the will of God, what is good and acceptable and perfect.

Only when you make yourself a living sacrifice, saying "Yes, Lord," even before you have heard your assignment, can you be clear about his will. As long as you negotiate your obedience, he is unlikely to reveal his will.[2]

Grow in Intimacy with Christ

As you try your best to be a living sacrifice, you can grow in your knowledge of Christ, learning to recognize his voice. John White writes about "guidance" in his book, *The Fight*,[3] saying, "Though the Bible never uses the word guidance, it does talk about a Guide. You may seek guidance, but God desires to give something better: himself." As you walk with Christ and get to know him better, your ability to discern his voice sharpens. You learn what pleases him. Jesus said, "My sheep hear my voice" (John 10.27).

Jesus sent the Counselor, the Holy Spirit, to teach us all things and remind us of everything Jesus said (John 14.26). He leads us in making God-honoring decisions, but also comforts us in our distress. We have a Guide who gives both direction and comfort.

Once you understand the overall kingdom purpose of God, you can live out your Christian life within that purpose. As you continue to grow in intimate knowledge of God, through trust in the Holy Spirit, there are some concrete things to consider in discerning God's will for your specific situation.

Apply Scripture
Your primary source of guidance should come from Scripture.

> All Scripture is breathed out by God and profitable for teaching, for reproof, for correction, and for training in righteousness, that the man of God may be competent, equipped for every good work.
> ~ 2 Timothy 3.16-17

Most questions are already answered in the Bible. "How can a young man keep his way pure? By guarding it according to your word. I have stored up your word in my heart, that I might not sin against you" (Ps. 119.9, 11). It is essential to be diligent in your study of the Word in order to know his mind.

Discern Your Passions
While God can reveal his will in a direct way, as he did with many of the biblical characters like Moses and Noah, he often reveals his will through the passions we develop for ministry. David built the temple out of his own heart for God. Hezekiah organized a large Passover celebration,

motivated by his gratitude toward God. You can develop hundreds of innovative ways to worship God and make him known. Take your creative passions seriously.

Pay Attention to Discontent
An especially important sign is persistent discontent with an existing situation. Remember David's words about the temple: "See now, I dwell in a house of cedar, but the ark of God dwells in a tent" (2 Sam. 7.2). Your unrest with the present state of affairs may be a good indication of something God wants to do through you.

Use Your Gifts
God gifts all believers for works of service, to build up the body (Rom. 12.3-8, 1 Cor. 12, Eph. 4.11-13). While God is the Giver of gifts and can give anyone new gifts at any time, you typically will be guided into projects based on your past gifting. God will use your gifts to accomplish his task. You can often recognize God's guiding hand if it involves something within your gifting.

Listen to Spiritual Authority
Having placed yourself under authority of a church body, pay careful attention to their leadership. You need to submit to their authority since they are responsible for your well-being.

> Obey your leaders and submit to them, for they are keeping watch over your souls, as those who will

have to give an account. Let them do this with joy and not with groaning, for that would be of no advantage to you.

~ Hebrews 13.17

If you have a vision for ministry and your leaders do not confirm God's leading in it, you need to pay careful attention to this "red flag." God is able to make his will known through the affirmation (or lack of affirmation) of godly leaders over you.

Receive Counsel from the Body

You can easily deceive yourself about your own motives. You can trick yourself into thinking something is of God when it really comes from your own desires, even if the idea seems selfless. You may "feel a peace" about something after time of prayer or fasting. But you can still fool yourself into doing what you want, even after sincere prayer and reflection on God's Word. That is why you need the input of brothers and sisters who know you well, and can separate out your intentions. "The heart is deceitful above all things, and desperately sick" (Jer. 17.9). "No one does good, not even one" (Rom. 3.12).

Seek out counsel before making a decision. "Without counsel plans fail, but with many advisers they succeed" (Prov. 15.22). Your friends can have great insight to help you discern God's will.

When you consider counsel from another, remember that you are making the final decision. You are responsible for your own actions. You should not "blame" the counselor for their advice. Make the choice and live with the outcome.

Observe Circumstances

Many people look at circumstances and say, "It must be God's will–look what is happening." Be very careful about basing God's guidance on circumstances alone. Circumstances ought to be the last, and least, of all the measures to discern God's will. His will may be to go completely against the grain of current circumstances. A closed door may mean you need to persevere to open it. An open door could be a tempting distraction.

Consider the Confirmation of Others

Sometimes confirmation comes from non-believers who give a wise word of counsel. God can speak even through non-Christians, or secular sources. But you should be careful to discern whether this is confirmation of biblical counsel or just worldly advice.

Learn from Past Experience

Much of your experience in discerning God's will, and hearing his voice, comes through years of learning from your mistakes. When you act on something, God can reveal, in hindsight, that you were really acting out of your own motivations, rather than God's. But he is gentle with you, using those opportunities to help you grow. Because God can redeem your mistakes, you should be bold in trying things for him. Do not let fear rule you.

Trusting God to guide you, even through your mistakes, is the key to discerning his will. "Trust in the Lord with all your heart, and do not lean on your own understanding. In all your ways acknowledge him, and he will make straight your paths." (Prov. 3.5-6).

You can have confidence that he will give you wisdom. "If any of you lacks wisdom, let him ask God, who gives generously to all without reproach, and it will be given him" (James 1.5).

Understand the big picture, be a living sacrifice, grow in intimacy with Christ, applying Scripture to your situation. Discern your passions, paying attention to your discontent, and use your spiritual gifts. Pay attention to spiritual authority and receive counsel from the body. Observe the circumstances of the situation and consider the reconfirmation of others. Learn from your past experience and be released to the joy of being set on fire for the Lord.

For Further Reading
Henry Blackaby's *Experiencing God*[4] outlines a lifestyle of recognizing God's leading.

Notes

[1] Ladd, George. 1959. *The Gospel of the Kingdom*. Grand Rapids, MI: Eerdmans.

[2] Jonah is a notable exception. But the story of Jonah exemplifies how God is able to discipline us to the point of obedience to his leading. Notice that God did not send Jonah until Jonah surrendered to God in the belly of the great fish (Jonah 2). Then Jonah was vomited onto dry ground where he was given another chance to set off to Nineveh (Jon. 3.1).

[3] White, John. 1976. *The Fight*. Downers Grove, IL: InterVarsity Press, page 154.

[4] Blackaby, Henry, and Claude King. 1990. *Experiencing God*. Nashville, TN: LifeWay Press. His main points are:

- ⬦ God is always at work around you.
- ⬦ God pursues a continuing love relationship with you that is real and personal.
- ⬦ God invites you to become involved with him in his work.
- ⬦ God speaks by the Holy Spirit through the Bible, prayer, circumstances, and the Church to reveal himself, his purposes, and his ways.
- ⬦ God's invitation for you to work with him always leads you to a crisis of belief that requires faith and action.
- ⬦ You must make major adjustments in your life to join God in what he is doing.

What If I Have No Passion?

THE SINGLE greatest aspect of leadership is passion to lead others toward the vision. The simple truth is: no passion, no leadership. No amount of wisdom, planning, or cleverness will make up for a lack of passion. Without passion, the endeavor will fall short.

As a leader, you must have a single-minded focus on the vision; a consistent energy that drives you toward the task.

Passion will force you to come up with innovative ways to progress toward the vision. Passion is the source of innovation. It is this inner drive that causes thirst for the wisdom that leads to effectiveness. But what if you find yourself lacking passion and motivation?

Praise

Without question, the single greatest way to increase your passion is to practice a persistent attitude of praise.[2] Praise turns your attention from thinking about yourself and focuses your mind on who God is. Praise is the reason you were created. When you praise, you live out your highest purpose. Praise allows God to renew your spirit and passion. When you praise, you are in a position to receive the knowledge of God, filling you with joy to overflowing, despite your circumstances.

Ask God
Ask God for renewed passion. "How much more will your Father who is in heaven give good things to those who ask him!" (Matt. 7.11). "Blessed are those who hunger and thirst for righteousness, for they shall be satisfied" (Matt. 5.6).

Ask God if there is any broken relationship with him that might cause your love for him to grow cold (Rev. 2.4).

The Basics
Always watch for the basics: are you getting enough sleep and exercise? Simple health matters can make a significant difference in how you view your life and ministry.

If you have asked God for passion, and have checked your life for sin that would block your relationship with God, continue being obedient to what you know. Wait for the passion to come. Many times, God's people go through temporary spiritual dry spells that distort their knowledge of the Lord. God desires for us to persevere even when we do not feel like it.

Peter's Prescription

2 Peter 1.3-7 outlines the process that keeps you from being "ineffective and unproductive" in your knowledge of our Lord Jesus:

> His divine power has granted to us all things that pertain to life and godliness, through the knowledge of him who called us to his own glory and excellence, by which he has granted to us his precious and very great promises, so that through them you may become partakers of the divine nature, having escaped from the corruption that is in the world because of sinful desire. For this very reason, make every effort to supplement your faith with virtue, and virtue with knowledge, and knowledge with self-control, and self-control with steadfastness, and steadfastness with godliness, and godliness with brotherly affection, and brotherly affection with love.

When you hit a dry spot, you should push ahead, seeking faith, goodness, knowledge, self-control, perseverance, godliness, brotherly kindness, and love.

As you walk in obedience to Christ, passion and emotion will follow your obedience. "But seek first the kingdom of God and his righteousness, and all these things will be added to you" (Matt. 6.33). You can be set on fire again.

Notes

[2] Davis, Dr. Don. 2003. *School for Urban Cross Cultural Church Planting.* Wichita, KS: World Impact Press.

Vision versus Goals:
How Are They Different?

What then is Apollos? What is Paul? Servants through whom you believed, as the Lord assigned to each. I planted, Apollos watered, but God gave the growth. So neither he who plants nor he who waters is anything, but only God who gives the growth. He who plants and he who waters are one, and each will receive his wages according to his labor.

~ 1 Corinthians 3.5-8

VISION IS a picture of what God puts on your heart. Goals are the things you do in response. There are things that God does, but he also chooses to use your efforts to accomplish his tasks.

Man plants and waters, but God make things grow. God plants churches, but man evangelizes, equips and empowers through various projects. Man cares for the plant until it can exist on its own, but God determines the growth.

One danger is that you can over-spiritualize, minimize the role you play, and "put everything in God's hands." The other danger is that you can put too much emphasis on your own effort and wisdom and forge ahead without God.

Once you have developed a vision for a project, you construct specific action steps to see that vision come to reality. These action steps are called *goals*.

For example, if your project is to perform a wedding, you have a picture in your mind, a vision, of what will happen. Then, in response to that vision, you take steps to make it reality. You construct a message, determine the order of service, assign someone to host the bride and her party, etc.

These goals are steps you take toward the vision. The ultimate result is beyond your control, but you take responsibility for the things you *can* control.

God accomplishes vision. You respond to vision by pursuing goals.

Person	Task	Situation When Called	Message/ Messenger
Noah Genesis 6-9	Build ark and save all living creatures	500-600 years old	Direct from God
Abraham Genesis 12-22	Leave country and go to a place God shows; believe God for promise to make a great nation; sacrifice son at Moriah	75 years old	God in a vision
Joseph Genesis 37-50	Save Israel from famine as governor of Egypt	A boy	Dream foretold his destiny; later interpreting dreams as a slave in prison
Moses Exodus 2-14	Lead Israel out of Egyptian bondage	Fugitive shepherd in the desert	God in a burning bush
Moses Numbers 1, 26	Conduct a census with help from tribal leaders	Leader of Israel	Direct from God
Moses Exodus 25-31	Construct Tabernacle and Ark	Leader of Israel	Direct from God

Person	Task	Situation When Called	Message/ Messenger
12 Spies Numbers 13-14	Explore the land God was giving to Israel	Leaders in each tribe	God through Moses
Joshua Joshua 1-24	Conquest of Canaan	2nd in command under Moses	Directly from God
Joshua Joshua 2-6	Conquest of Jericho	Newly appointed leader of Israel	Angel
Deborah and Barak Judges 4	Defeat Jabin's army and King of Canaan with 10,000 men	Prophetess and Leader of Israel	From God through the Prophetess/ Judge
Gideon Judges 6-8	Save Israel from Midian	Threshing wheat	Angel
Jephthah Judges 11-12	Defeat Ammonites	In exile for being born of a prostitute	Through the invitation of leaders
Samson Judges 13-16	Defeat Philistines	Set apart at birth	Angel
David 1 Samuel 17	Defeat Goliath	Lowly shepherd when anointed king; not yet revealed	Own passion

Person	Task	Situation When Called	Message/ Messenger
David and Solomon 2 Samuel 7; 1 Kings 5-9; 1 Chronicles 22, 28	Build the temple	King of Israel	Own passion
Hezekiah 2 Chronicles 29.1-31.1	Celebrate Passover to commemorate restoration of the temple	King of Israel	Own passion
Jehoash and Jehoida 2 Kings 12	Repair the temple	King and Priest of Israel	Own passion
Esther Esther 1-10	Save Israel from extinction	Orphan in exile	Through her leader and circumstances
Cyrus and Zerubbabel Ezra 1-10, Haggai 1-2; Zechariah 1-14	Rebuild the temple	In exile	King Cyrus was moved by Jeremiah's prophecy
Nehemiah Nehemiah 1-13	Rebuild the wall of Jerusalem	In exile as cupbearer to the king	Own passion
Jonah Jonah 1-5	Preach to Ninevites	Prophet	God

Person	Task	Situation When Called	Message/ Messenger
Mary and Joseph Matthew 1, Luke 1	Raise the Messiah	Young Nazarene engaged couple	Angel (Mary) Angel in a dream (Joseph)
Joseph Matthew 2	Flee to Egypt and return at a later time	Young husband and father	Angel in dream
72 Disciples Luke 10.1-17	Preach the Good News	Followers of Jesus	Jesus
Jesus 1 John 3.8; Gospels; Eph. 3.11-12; Col. 1.13-14	Destroy the works of the devil; suffer and die on our behalf	Born into an obscure Jewish carpenter's family in a Bethlehem stable	The Father
Paul and Barnabas Acts 8; 13.1-3	Mission to Asia Minor; broken into a number of separate missionary journeys	Church planting in Antioch (former persecutor of the Church)	Holy Spirit through prophetic word
Philip Acts 8.26-40	Go to Gaza road	Deacon of the Jerusalem church	Angel
Peter Acts 10	Preach to Cornelius (Gentiles)	Leading apostle in Jerusalem	Vision

Person	Task	Situation When Called	Message/ Messenger
Paul and Barnabas Acts 11.27-30	Send offering to church in Judea	Leaders in Antioch church	Holy Spirit via prophetic word and leaders' own initiative
Apostles Matthew 28.8-10	Great Commission	Apostles	Jesus

Developing
Habits of Wisdom

LIKE OTHER skills, you can improve in your ability to be wise. Although wisdom is a gift from God, you should also be a good steward by working hard to develop your wisdom.

The table below lists fifteen key questions, covering six principles, that are useful whenever you go through the process of decision making, problem solving, or designing ministry projects. The more you utilize these questions, the more effective you will become. These questions are a slight modification from the work of Christian Schwartz's work in *Natural Church Development*.[1]

Principle:
    Chain Reaction (1 Cor. 12, the body)
Characteristic:
    Sensitive
Description:
    Ministries are interconnected to each other; changes in one will affect others
Key Questions:
    1. What are some unintended consequences?
    2. What are the short-term and long-term implications?

Principle:

Reproducibility (John 12.24, "unless a grain of wheat falls into the earth and dies, it remains alone; but if it dies, it bears much fruit.")

Characteristic:

Visionary

Description:

Healthy organisms don't grow endlessly but reproduce themselves

Key Questions:

1. Is there a way to do this that contributes to multiplication instead of just addition?

2. Can we look at producing a group rather than an individual?

Principle:

Redemptive (Acts 17, Paul and the "unknown god")

Characteristic:

Opportunistic

Description:

Use energy (positive and negative) to accomplish God's purposes

Key Questions:

1. How can we use a bad situation and turn it to an opportunity?

2. How can we build on the momentum of a good situation?

3. Are we using forces or fighting against them?

Principle:

Two birds, one stone (Exod. 18, the Jethro principle)

Characteristic:

Efficient

Description:

Try to accomplish multiple purposes with one effort (e.g. do ministry AND develop leaders)

Key Questions:

1. Since we are spending energy to do this, what other goals could we accomplish simultaneously?

2. What can we do ONCE that will minimize doing the same thing repeatedly?

Principle:

Win-win (1 Sam. 20, David and Jonathan)

Characteristic:

Synergistic

Description:

Dissimilar organisms working together are mutually beneficial (e.g. rhino and bird)

Key Questions:

1. How can dissimilar people or ministries work together toward this goal or problem?

2. How do we promote cooperation and minimize competition?

3. How might dissimilar people or ministries benefit by working together?

Principle:

 Fruit checking (John 15, the Vine and the branches)

Characteristic:

 Effective

Description:

 Check the fruit for pruning, removing, or cultivating

Key Questions:

 1. What is the intended result?

 2. How can we make sure time and effort contribute toward the desired result (rather than just activity for activity's sake)?

 3. To get the desired results, what should we abandon? Retain? Add?

---

1. What are some unintended consequences?
2. What are the short-term and long-term implications?
3. Is there a way to do this that contributes to multiplication instead of just addition?
4. Can we look at producing a group rather than an individual?
5. How can we use a bad situation and turn it to an opportunity?
6. How can we build on the momentum of a good situation?
7. Are we using forces or fighting against them?
8. Since we are spending energy to do this, what other goals could we accomplish simultaneously?
9. What can we do ONCE that will minimize doing the same thing repeatedly?
10. How can dissimilar people or ministries work together toward this goal or problem?
11. How do we promote cooperation and minimize competition?

12. How might dissimilar people or ministries benefit by working together?
13. What is the intended result?
14. How can we make sure time and effort contribute toward the desired result (rather than just activity for activity's sake)?
15. To get the desired results, what should we abandon? Retain? Add?

Different people with different personalities and spiritual gifts tend to emphasize various principles. Those who are especially sensitive to others will be more in tune to the "Chain Reaction" principle, while those who are entrepreneurial will gravitate toward the "Redemptive" principle. Depending on the magnitude of your project or decision, it is wise to seek counsel from people who are especially gifted in each of these principles, in order to get a full picture of the implications of your decision.

Notes

[1] Schwartz, Christian. 1998. *Natural Church Development.* Carol Stream, IL: ChurchSmart Resources.

World Impact and
The Urban Ministry Institute

World Impact

World Impact is a Christian missions organization dedicated to ministering God's love in the inner cities of America. Our purpose is to honor and glorify God and delight in him in the inner cities by knowing God and making him known. World Impact ministers cross-culturally to people unreached by the Gospel of Jesus Christ through evangelism, follow-up, discipleship and indigenous church planting. World Impact empowers urban disciples; training leadership for the advancement of the Kingdom of God. Our ministry is:

Incarnational: Our missionaries live in the communities where they minister.

Evangelical: We present Christ to the unchurched through Bible clubs, Bible studies and worship services.

Discipleship-oriented: We nurture people to maturity in Christ and train them to teach others.

Compassionate: We demonstrate the Gospel we declare by providing:

✧ *Christian elementary and middle schools*

- ◇ *Emergency food, clothing, medicine and shelter*
- ◇ *Christian camping and retreats*
- ◇ *Job training*
- ◇ *Tutoring*
- ◇ *Sports and recreation programs*
- ◇ *Medical and dental clinics*

Contact Us:

www.worldimpact.org
2001 South Vermont Ave
Los Angeles, CA 90007
323-735-1137
323-735-2576 (fax)
info@worldimpact.org

The Urban Ministry Institute

The Urban Ministry Institute is a training institution that exists to equip leaders for the urban church, especially among the poor, in order to advance the Kingdom of God.

Equips Leaders

Although we live in a culture where leaders are openly disrespected and the idea of leadership is seen as oppressive, we believe that leaders are of fundamental importance, especially in the life of God's Church. Leaders may be formal or informal, pastors or lay leaders, men or women. They may be mothers or fathers, evangelists, missionaries, Sunday School teachers, worship leaders or those who visit the sick. We are interested in anyone whom

God has gifted and called to lead in his or her church at any level of responsibility.

For the Urban Church

Believing strongly that effective ministry cannot take place apart from the body of Christ, The Urban Ministry Institute is committed to enriching the outreach of urban congregations and their servant-leaders. All of our programs and materials are designed to equip men and women to serve in the context of a local assembly.

Half of the people alive today live in cities, and that number is constantly growing. This calls for a special focus on urban churches, especially in those areas which have historically been neglected, or have large concentrations of people who have not been reached with the Gospel of Christ.

Especially Among the Poor

We believe that God has "chosen those who are poor in the world to be rich in faith and heirs of the kingdom, which he has promised to those who love him" (James 2.5). Whether you are rich, poor, or somewhere in-between, we believe that Jesus has given all believers a theological mandate to prioritize the poor in their life and ministry.

God is raising up leaders who will go to the unreached millions among the urban poor both in America and around the world. All of them deserve access to quality theological education.

In Order to Advance the Kingdom of God
The Church of Jesus Christ is the agent of the Kingdom of God, charged to function as salt and light in the midst of a decaying and corrupt world. The freedom, wholeness, and justice of the Kingdom of God is to be embodied and proclaimed by the Church. A church community is responsible to show what the "Rule of God" looks like as it embraces people who acknowledge Christ's lordship. The Urban Ministry Institute is dedicated to helping churches make God's reign visible in all the dimensions of Christian community life.

Contact Us:

www.tumi.org
3701 E. 13th Street Wichita, Kansas 67208
info@tumi.org
316-681-1317
316-681-1316 (fax)

Works Cited

Ambrose, Stephen. 1996. *Undaunted Courage*. New York: Simon and Schuster.

Baker, Sunny and Kim. 1998. *The Complete Idiot's Guide to Project Management*. New York: Macmillan Publishing.

Barna, George. 1992. *The Power of Vision*. Ventura, CA: Regal Books.

Blackaby, Henry, and Claude King. 1990. *Experiencing God*. Nashville, TN: LifeWay Press.

Buckingham, Marcus. 2005. *The One Thing You Need to Know*. New York, NY: Free Press.

Burns, Ken. 1997. *Lewis and Clark: The Journey of the Corps of Discovery*. Burbank, CA: PBS Home Video.

Charlton, James, ed. 2002. *The Military Quotation Book*. New York: St. Martin's Press.

Collins, Jim. 2001. *Good to Great*. New York, NY: HarperCollins Publishers.

Davis, Don. 2003. *School for Urban Cross Cultural Church Planting*. Wichita, KS: World Impact Press.

------. 2005. *World Impact Focus and Identity*. Lake Hughes, CA: World Impact Press.

DePree, Max. 1989. *Leadership Is an Art*. New York, NY: Dell Publishing.

Easum, Bill. 1997. *Growing Spiritual Redwoods*. Nashville, TN: Abingdon.

Fast Company. March 2001. "Seven Secrets of Good Brainstorming." www.fastcompany.com/ change/change_feature/kelley.html

Goodstein, Leonard, Timothy Nolan, and J. William Pfeiffer. 1993. *Applied Strategic Planning*. New York, NY: McGraw-Hill.

Gothard, Bill. 1979. *Basic Seminar Textbook*. Oak Brook, IL: Institute for Basic Youth Conflicts.

Hammonds, Keith H. June 2002. *The Strategy of the Fighter Pilot*. Fast Company.

Howard, Ron. 1995. *Apollo 13*. http://www.scottlondon.com/insight/ scripts/wheatley.html. Burbank, CA: MCA Universal Pictures.

Insight and Outlook. November 1996. "The New Science of Leadership: An Interview with Margaret Wheatley." http://www.scott london.com/insight/scripts/wheatley.html.

Kennedy, John F. May 25, 1961. *Special Message to the Congress on Urgent National Needs*.

Labovitz, George, and Victor Rosansky. 1997. *The Power of Alignment: How Great Companies Stay Centered and Accomplish Extraordinary Things*. New York, NY: John Wiley & Sons, Inc.

Ladd, George. 1959. *The Gospel of the Kingdom*. Grand Rapids, MI: Eerdmans.

McCarthy, E. Jerome. 1981. *Basic Marketing: A Managerial Approach*. 7th ed. Homewood, IL: Richard D. Irwin.

Mintzberg, Henry. 1994. *The Rise and Fall of Strategic Planning*. New York, NY: The Free Press.

Mrazek, James. 1968. *The Art of Winning Wars*. New York, NY: Walker Books.

NetFax. March-April 1999. http://www.ntcumc.org/ArcMyC/MyC9903.html.

Salvendy, Gavriel, editor. 1982. *Handbook of Industrial Engineering*. New York: John Wiley and Sons, Inc.

Schwartz, Christian. 1998. *Natural Church Development*. Carol Stream, IL: ChurchSmart Resources.

Welch, Jack. September 2005. *The Five Stages of Crisis Management*. Opinion Journal. www.opinionjournal.com/feature.html?id=11000 7256.

Wheatley, Margaret. 1992. *Leadership and the New Science*. San Francisco: Berrett Koehler.

White, John. 1976. *The Fight*. Downers Grove, IL: InterVarsity Press.